Category Management in Purchasing

Strategies, Tools, and Best Practices

Table of Contents

Introduction to Category Management — 5
   What is Category Management? — 6
   Its Importance in Modern Procurement — 7
   Objectives and Scope of the Book — 8
Chapter 1: The Concept of Category Management — 12
   Definition and Key Principles — 13
   The Evolution of Procurement and Role of Category Management — 14
   Benefits of Adopting a Category Approach — 15
Chapter 2: The Category Management Framework — 18
   Overview of the Category Management Process — 19
   Key Elements: Strategy, Tools, and Stakeholder Involvement — 20
   How Category Management Differs from Traditional Procurement — 22
Chapter 3: Organizational Readiness for Category Management — 26
   Assessing Current Procurement Maturity — 27
   Building a Category Management Capability — 28
   Roles and Responsibilities in Category Teams — 30
Chapter 4: Spend Analysis and Data Management — 32
   Importance of Spend Analysis in Category Management — 32
   Tools and Techniques for Analyzing Spend Data — 33
   Identifying Opportunities from Data Insights — 35
Chapter 5: Understanding Supply Markets — 39
   Conducting Supplier and Market Analysis — 40
   Key Tools: Porter's Five Forces, SWOT, and PESTLE Analysis — 41
   Identifying Market Trends and Supply Chain Risks — 45
Chapter 6: Segmenting Categories for Maximum Value — 46
   Category Segmentation and Prioritization — 47
   Kraljic Matrix and Strategic Sourcing Models — 48
   Tailoring Strategies for Different Categories — 50
Chapter 7: Developing Category Strategies — 53
   Defining Objectives and Goals for Each Category — 54
   Aligning Strategies with Organizational Goals — 55
   Balancing Cost, Quality, and Risk — 56
8. Supplier Relationship Management (SRM) — 60
   Building Strategic Relationships with Key Suppliers — 61
   Collaborative vs. Transactional Approaches — 62
   Tools for SRM: Scorecards, Dashboards, and Relationship Mapping — 63
Chapter 9: Procurement and Negotiation Strategies — 68
   Advanced Negotiation Techniques for Category Managers — 69

    Total Cost of Ownership (TCO) vs. Price Focus   71
    Managing Contract Lifecycles   72
Chapter 10: Implementing Category Plans   **75**
    Transitioning from Strategy to Execution   76
    Effective Communication and Stakeholder Alignment   77
    Tracking Milestones and Deliverables   79
Chapter 11: Measuring and Managing Performance   **81**
    Defining Key Performance Indicators (KPIs) for Categories   81
    Tools for Monitoring and Reporting Category Performance   83
    Continuous Improvement through Feedback Loops   85
Chapter 12: Risk Management in Categories   **87**
    Identifying and Managing Procurement Risks   88
    Building Resilience in Category Strategies   91
    Case Studies in Effective Risk Mitigation   92
Chapter 13: Role of Digital Transformation   **95**
    Procurement 4.0 and Its Impact on Category Management   96
    Leveraging Big Data, AI, and Machine Learning   97
    Tools for Digital Category Management   99
    The Future of Digital Category Management   101
Chapter 14: Automating Category Management   **103**
    Benefits of Automation in Procurement Processes   104
    Examples: e-Procurement, Spend Analytics, and Category Dashboards   106
    Overcoming Challenges in Automation   108
Chapter 15: Sustainable and Ethical Sourcing   **110**
    Incorporating Sustainability into Category Strategies   111
    Ethical Procurement Practices: Avoiding Modern Slavery and Corruption   113
    Measuring and Reporting on Sustainability Goals   114
Chapter 16: Category Management in Different Industries   **117**
    Manufacturing and Raw Materials   118
    Retail and Consumer Goods   119
    Pharmaceuticals and Healthcare   121
Chapter 17: Global Category Management   **123**
    Managing Categories in Multi-Regional Environments   123
    Adapting to Local Markets and Regulations   125
    Best Practices for Global Sourcing   126
Chapter 18: Collaboration Across the Organization   **129**
    Role of Cross-Functional Teams in Category Success   129
    Building Partnerships with Finance, Legal, and Operations   130
    Overcoming Internal Resistance to Change   133
Chapter 19: Future Trends in Category Management   **136**
    Agile Procurement and Category Management   137
    The Growing Role of Analytics and Predictive Insights   138
    Integrating Technology and Data-Driven Decision-Making   140
    Emerging Challenges and Opportunities in Category Management   142

20. Building a Culture of Continuous Improvement in Category Management 149
    Learning from Successes and Failures   150
    Embedding Category Management in Organizational Culture   152
    The Evolving Role of the Category Manager   153
Glossary of Key Terms   **156**
    Practical Tools and Templates   157
    Real-World Case Studies   158
    References and Further Reading   160

Introduction to Category Management

Category Management has emerged as a transformative approach in modern procurement, reshaping the way organizations manage their supply chains and procurement strategies. It is not merely a process but a philosophy that focuses on treating product and service categories as strategic business units. This approach goes beyond transactional buying, aiming to unlock value, drive efficiency, and align procurement objectives with the broader goals of the organization. To fully appreciate its significance and potential, it is crucial to delve into its definition, understand its importance in the contemporary procurement landscape, and explore the objectives and scope that make it a cornerstone of strategic sourcing.

What is Category Management?

Category Management is a strategic approach to procurement that organizes purchasing activities around specific categories of goods or services. A category, in this context, refers to a group of products or services that share similar characteristics or fulfill similar needs. Instead of managing procurement on an ad-hoc or fragmented basis, Category Management involves treating each category as a distinct business unit, complete with tailored strategies that maximize value for the organization.

The essence of Category Management lies in its emphasis on understanding the nuances of each category, including supply market dynamics, supplier capabilities, and customer requirements. It involves conducting in-depth analysis, segmenting spend, and developing category-specific strategies that address cost, quality, risk, and sustainability. By shifting the focus from individual transactions to a holistic view of categories, organizations can achieve greater control, better supplier relationships, and more significant cost efficiencies.

Its Importance in Modern Procurement

In today's highly competitive and globalized business environment, procurement has evolved from a back-office function to a strategic enabler of organizational success. Category Management plays a pivotal role in this transformation by providing a structured framework for procurement activities that align with organizational objectives.

One of the key reasons for the growing importance of Category Management is its ability to deliver cost savings. Through detailed spend analysis and strategic sourcing, organizations can identify cost drivers, leverage economies of scale, and negotiate more favorable terms with suppliers. However, the impact of Category Management extends far beyond cost savings. It fosters innovation by encouraging collaboration with suppliers, enhances risk management by identifying vulnerabilities within supply chains, and supports sustainability by integrating ethical and environmental considerations into procurement decisions.

Furthermore, Category Management helps organizations navigate the complexities of global supply chains. With supply markets becoming increasingly dynamic and interconnected, a one-size-fits-all approach to procurement is no longer sufficient. Category Management allows organizations to tailor their strategies to the unique challenges and opportunities of each category, ensuring agility and resilience in the face of market disruptions.

Another critical aspect of its importance lies in its ability to drive value creation. By focusing on total cost of ownership (TCO) rather than just upfront costs, Category Management ensures that procurement decisions deliver long-term benefits. It also enables organizations to align their procurement activities with customer needs, thereby enhancing the overall value proposition.

Objectives and Scope of the Book

The primary objective of this book is to provide a comprehensive guide to Category Management, equipping readers with the knowledge and tools they need to implement this approach effectively within their organizations. Whether you are a procurement professional, a supply chain manager, or a business leader, this book aims to offer valuable insights that will help you unlock the full potential of Category Management.

One of the fundamental goals of this book is to demystify the concept of Category Management. While the term is widely used in procurement circles, its practical implementation often remains misunderstood or poorly executed. By breaking down the principles and practices of Category Management into actionable steps, this book seeks to bridge the gap between theory and practice.

Another objective is to highlight the strategic importance of Category Management in achieving organizational goals. This book will explore how Category Management can drive cost savings, enhance supplier relationships, and contribute to broader business objectives such as innovation, sustainability, and risk mitigation. Through real-world examples and case studies, readers will gain a deeper understanding of how leading organizations have leveraged Category Management to achieve competitive advantage.

The scope of this book extends to all aspects of Category Management, from foundational concepts to advanced techniques. It begins with an exploration of the fundamental principles of Category Management, including its definition, benefits, and role in modern procurement. Subsequent chapters delve into the step-by-step process of implementing Category Management, covering key activities such as spend analysis, market research, category strategy development, and supplier management.

In addition to the core processes, this book addresses emerging trends and challenges in Category Management. With the rapid advancement of technology and the growing emphasis on sustainability, the field of procurement is undergoing significant changes. This book examines how tools like artificial intelligence, big data analytics, and blockchain are shaping the future of Category Management. It also explores the increasing importance of ethical and sustainable sourcing, offering practical guidance on integrating these considerations into category strategies.

Another critical area of focus is the organizational aspect of Category Management. Effective implementation requires collaboration across departments, alignment with corporate goals, and the development of specialized skills. This book provides insights into building a Category Management capability within an organization, including tips on stakeholder engagement, team structure, and performance measurement.

Finally, the book aims to serve as a practical resource for professionals at all levels of experience. For those new to Category Management, it offers a clear and concise introduction to the concept and its benefits. For experienced practitioners, it provides advanced strategies, tools, and techniques to enhance existing practices. Regardless of your level of expertise, this book is designed to help you achieve better outcomes in procurement and drive value for your organization.

By focusing on these aspects, the book sets the stage for a deep dive into the intricacies of Category Management, ensuring that readers have a solid foundation to build upon. This introduction not only defines what Category Management is but also underscores its critical role in modern procurement and outlines the comprehensive approach that the book will take to address this vital subject.

Chapter 1: The Concept of Category Management

Definition and Key Principles

Category Management is a strategic approach to procurement that involves grouping products or services into distinct categories based on similar characteristics, supply markets, or usage within an organization. Each category is treated as a separate business unit, with a tailored strategy aimed at maximizing value, minimizing costs, and mitigating risks. This method is a departure from traditional procurement practices that often focus solely on price negotiations and transactional relationships with suppliers.

At its core, Category Management revolves around the principle of achieving total cost optimization rather than simply reducing upfront purchase costs. It takes a holistic view of the procurement process, incorporating elements such as supplier relationship management, market analysis, risk assessment, and sustainability. By leveraging data and insights, it enables organizations to align their procurement strategies with broader corporate objectives, fostering innovation, efficiency, and competitive advantage.

Key principles that underpin Category Management include:

- **Segmentation:** Dividing procurement into categories to focus on specific market dynamics and supplier capabilities.
- **Strategic Planning:** Developing customized strategies for each category based on thorough analysis and stakeholder alignment.
- **Collaboration:** Promoting cross-functional collaboration to align procurement activities with organizational goals.
- **Value Creation:** Focusing on delivering long-term value rather than short-term cost savings.

- **Continuous Improvement:** Emphasizing ongoing evaluation and optimization of category strategies.

These principles ensure that Category Management remains a dynamic and results-driven approach, capable of adapting to the evolving needs of an organization and its supply chain.

The Evolution of Procurement and Role of Category Management

The field of procurement has undergone a significant transformation over the past few decades. Historically, procurement was viewed as a cost-centric function, primarily responsible for purchasing goods and services at the lowest possible price. This approach often lacked strategic alignment with broader business objectives and failed to account for the complexities of global supply chains.

With the advent of globalization and technological advancements, procurement evolved into a more strategic function. Organizations began recognizing the potential of procurement to drive innovation, improve efficiency, and create competitive advantages. This shift led to the adoption of advanced practices, including strategic sourcing, supplier relationship management, and ultimately, Category Management.

Category Management emerged as a response to the need for a more structured and strategic approach to procurement. It provided a framework for organizations to move beyond transactional buying and focus on optimizing entire categories of spend. By emphasizing a data-driven and analytical approach, Category Management enabled organizations to gain deeper insights into their spending patterns, supplier capabilities, and market dynamics.

The role of Category Management in modern procurement is multifaceted. It acts as a bridge between the procurement function and other business units, ensuring that purchasing decisions align with organizational goals. It also provides a mechanism for managing the complexities of global supply chains, allowing organizations to tailor their strategies to specific market conditions and supplier relationships.

Moreover, Category Management plays a critical role in addressing emerging challenges such as sustainability, risk management, and digital transformation. By integrating these elements into category strategies, organizations can not only enhance their procurement outcomes but also contribute to broader societal and environmental goals.

Benefits of Adopting a Category Approach

The adoption of a category-based approach to procurement offers numerous benefits, making it a valuable strategy for organizations across industries. These benefits extend beyond cost savings, encompassing aspects such as innovation, risk mitigation, and organizational efficiency.

> **Enhanced Cost Efficiency:**
> By analyzing spend data and leveraging economies of scale, Category Management enables organizations to achieve significant cost savings. This approach also considers the total cost of ownership (TCO), ensuring that procurement decisions deliver long-term financial benefits.
>
> **Improved Supplier Relationships:**
> Category Management emphasizes collaboration and partnership with key suppliers. By fostering strong relationships, organizations can unlock value through innovation, quality improvements, and better service

levels. Strategic partnerships also enhance supplier loyalty and reduce the risk of supply disruptions.

Risk Mitigation:
A category-based approach allows organizations to identify and address risks specific to each category. Whether it's supply chain disruptions, market volatility, or regulatory compliance, Category Management provides a framework for proactive risk management.

Alignment with Business Goals:
Category Management ensures that procurement activities are aligned with the overall objectives of the organization. This alignment enhances cross-functional collaboration and ensures that procurement contributes to strategic priorities such as revenue growth, market expansion, and customer satisfaction.

Enhanced Decision-Making:
The data-driven nature of Category Management enables more informed decision-making. By leveraging insights from spend analysis, market research, and supplier performance data, organizations can develop strategies that are both effective and adaptable to changing conditions.

Support for Sustainability Goals:
Category Management integrates sustainability considerations into procurement strategies, allowing organizations to reduce their environmental impact and promote ethical sourcing practices. This alignment with corporate social responsibility (CSR) objectives enhances the organization's reputation and stakeholder trust.

Scalability and Flexibility:
The structured framework of Category Management

makes it scalable across organizations of all sizes and industries. It also offers the flexibility to adapt to specific market conditions and business needs, ensuring its relevance in a rapidly changing global landscape.

Continuous Improvement:
By fostering a culture of continuous evaluation and optimization, Category Management ensures that procurement strategies remain effective over time. This focus on improvement drives innovation and keeps organizations ahead of the competition.

In conclusion, Category Management represents a paradigm shift in procurement, offering a strategic and holistic approach that aligns with the demands of modern business. By focusing on value creation, collaboration, and continuous improvement, it empowers organizations to achieve superior outcomes in cost efficiency, supplier relationships, and risk management. As procurement continues to evolve, the role of Category Management will only become more critical in driving organizational success.

Chapter 2: The Category Management Framework

Overview of the Category Management Process

The Category Management process is a structured, systematic approach to procurement that transforms how organizations source and manage goods and services. It focuses on grouping related products or services into categories, analyzing each category's market dynamics, and crafting tailored strategies to maximize value. The process is both iterative and collaborative, requiring cross-functional input and continuous refinement to adapt to changing business needs and market conditions.

At its core, the Category Management process involves several key stages:

Spend Analysis: This initial step involves collecting and analyzing data to understand the organization's spending patterns. The goal is to identify key spend categories, evaluate supplier performance, and uncover opportunities for cost savings or value creation.

Market Research: Understanding the supply market is critical for informed decision-making. This step involves analyzing market trends, supplier capabilities, competitive forces, and potential risks within the category.

Category Strategy Development: Based on the insights from spend analysis and market research, organizations create a comprehensive strategy for each category. This strategy aligns with organizational objectives and defines goals such as cost reduction, supplier innovation, or sustainability.

Supplier Selection and Relationship Management: Once the strategy is defined, the next step is to identify and engage with suppliers that align with the category objectives. This stage emphasizes fostering collaborative relationships to drive mutual value.

- **Implementation:** The strategy is put into action through detailed plans, contracts, and operational changes. Effective communication and stakeholder buy-in are crucial for successful execution.
- **Performance Measurement and Continuous Improvement:** Category Management is not a one-time effort. Regular performance reviews, supplier assessments, and strategy updates ensure that the process remains effective and evolves with changing circumstances.

By following this structured process, organizations can achieve greater alignment between their procurement activities and overall business goals. The process also enables organizations to anticipate and mitigate risks, capitalize on market opportunities, and drive long-term value creation.

Key Elements: Strategy, Tools, and Stakeholder Involvement

Category Management is underpinned by three critical elements that ensure its success: strategy, tools, and stakeholder involvement.

Strategy:
A robust strategy is the cornerstone of effective Category Management. It provides a clear roadmap for achieving category-specific objectives while aligning with broader organizational goals. A successful category strategy considers

multiple factors, including market conditions, supplier capabilities, and the organization's priorities. For instance, a strategy may focus on cost optimization, supplier innovation, risk reduction, or sustainability, depending on the category's importance and the organization's needs.

Strategic planning in Category Management also requires a long-term perspective. Instead of focusing solely on immediate cost savings, organizations must evaluate the total cost of ownership (TCO), lifecycle value, and potential future benefits. This forward-thinking approach ensures that procurement decisions contribute to sustainable growth and competitive advantage.

Tools:
Modern Category Management relies on a suite of tools and technologies that enable data-driven decision-making and process efficiency. Key tools include:

- **Spend Analysis Software:** Tools that consolidate and analyze spend data to uncover insights and trends.
- **Supplier Relationship Management (SRM) Platforms:** Systems that facilitate communication, collaboration, and performance tracking with suppliers.
- **Market Intelligence Platforms:** Tools that provide real-time insights into market trends, supplier landscapes, and emerging risks.
- **Contract Management Software:** Platforms that streamline contract creation, negotiation, and compliance monitoring.
- **Analytics and Reporting Tools:** Solutions that measure the performance of category strategies and identify areas for improvement.

The integration of digital technologies such as artificial intelligence (AI), machine learning, and big data analytics further enhances the capabilities of these tools, enabling predictive insights and automation.

Stakeholder Involvement:
The collaborative nature of Category Management requires active involvement from a diverse range of stakeholders. Procurement professionals, business unit leaders, finance teams, and even external suppliers play vital roles in the process.

Stakeholder involvement begins during the strategy development phase, where input from cross-functional teams ensures that category objectives align with organizational priorities. For example, engaging with marketing teams for indirect spend categories or involving operations for direct materials can provide valuable perspectives.

Equally important is maintaining open communication throughout the implementation and performance review stages. Clear communication fosters transparency, builds trust, and ensures that all parties are aligned on objectives and expectations.

How Category Management Differs from Traditional Procurement

While both Category Management and traditional procurement aim to secure goods and services for an organization, their approaches and outcomes differ significantly. Traditional procurement often focuses on transactional processes, emphasizing cost savings through competitive bidding and vendor negotiations. In contrast, Category Management takes a strategic, value-driven approach that considers long-term benefits and broader business objectives.

Key differences include:

Focus on Total Value:
Traditional procurement prioritizes upfront cost reduction, often at the expense of other considerations such as quality, risk, or sustainability. Category Management, on the other hand, emphasizes total value creation, which includes cost efficiency, innovation, and supplier collaboration.

Data-Driven Approach:
Category Management relies heavily on data analysis to inform decisions. Detailed spend analysis, market research, and performance metrics guide the development and execution of category strategies. Traditional procurement, in contrast, may rely more on historical practices or subjective judgment.

Supplier Relationships:
In traditional procurement, supplier relationships are often transactional, with limited collaboration or strategic engagement. Category Management fosters long-term partnerships with key suppliers, focusing on mutual value creation and innovation.

Strategic Alignment:
Category Management aligns procurement activities with organizational goals, such as revenue growth, market expansion, or sustainability. Traditional procurement operates more as a standalone function, with less emphasis on cross-functional alignment.

Process Orientation:
Traditional procurement tends to be reactive, addressing immediate purchasing needs as they arise. Category Management adopts a proactive, structured approach that anticipates future requirements and market changes.

By embracing the principles and practices of Category Management, organizations can transcend the limitations of traditional procurement and achieve superior outcomes in cost efficiency, supplier collaboration, and strategic alignment. This shift not only enhances the procurement function but also contributes to the organization's overall success in a dynamic and competitive business environment.

Chapter 3: Organizational Readiness for Category Management

Assessing Current Procurement Maturity

Before implementing Category Management, an organization must evaluate its current procurement maturity to determine its readiness for such a transformation. Procurement maturity reflects the sophistication, structure, and strategic alignment of the procurement function within an organization. This assessment serves as a baseline to identify gaps, strengths, and areas requiring development.

Organizations typically fall into one of three levels of procurement maturity:

1. **Transactional Procurement:** Procurement functions primarily focus on fulfilling immediate purchasing needs with limited strategic alignment. Processes are reactive, and cost savings are the primary metric of success.
2. **Strategic Sourcing:** Procurement begins to incorporate broader goals such as supplier relationship management and strategic planning. Processes are semi-structured, with some emphasis on total cost of ownership and risk management.
3. **Integrated Category Management:** The procurement function is fully aligned with organizational goals. It employs a category-driven approach, leveraging advanced tools, analytics, and cross-functional collaboration to create value beyond cost savings.

An organization can assess its procurement maturity using a combination of qualitative and quantitative methods. Key steps include:

- **Spend Analysis:** Evaluating procurement data to understand current spending patterns and supplier dependencies.
- **Process Review:** Analyzing existing procurement workflows to identify inefficiencies and bottlenecks.
- **Capability Assessment:** Evaluating the skills, knowledge, and tools available within the procurement team.
- **Stakeholder Feedback:** Gathering input from internal stakeholders to understand their expectations and perceptions of the procurement function.
- **Benchmarking:** Comparing procurement practices against industry standards and best practices to identify gaps.

The insights gained from this assessment guide the development of a roadmap for transitioning to Category Management. This roadmap typically includes process improvements, technology upgrades, and skill-building initiatives to enhance procurement maturity.

Building a Category Management Capability

Building a robust Category Management capability requires a deliberate and phased approach, focusing on people, processes, and technology. This transformation involves cultivating a strategic mindset, equipping teams with the necessary skills and tools, and fostering an organizational culture that supports collaboration and continuous improvement.

1. People:
The success of Category Management hinges on having the right talent in place. Procurement professionals must possess a blend of technical expertise and soft skills to execute category strategies effectively. Key skills include:

- **Analytical Thinking:** The ability to interpret data, conduct market research, and identify trends.
- **Negotiation:** Proficiency in negotiating contracts and managing supplier relationships.
- **Stakeholder Engagement:** Strong communication and collaboration skills to align category goals with business objectives.
- **Strategic Planning:** The capacity to develop and execute long-term category strategies.

Organizations can build these skills through targeted training programs, certifications, and mentorship. Additionally, hiring professionals with expertise in specific categories can enhance the team's capabilities.

2. Processes:

Establishing clear and efficient processes is essential for implementing Category Management. Organizations must:

- Define standard operating procedures (SOPs) for key activities such as spend analysis, strategy development, and supplier management.
- Develop templates and tools to streamline workflows and ensure consistency.
- Create performance metrics to track the effectiveness of category strategies and identify areas for improvement.

Process standardization reduces ambiguity, enhances accountability, and ensures that Category Management practices are applied uniformly across the organization.

3. Technology:

Advanced technology is a cornerstone of effective Category Management. Organizations should invest in tools that enable data analysis, supplier management, and market intelligence. Key technologies include:

- Spend analysis platforms to consolidate and analyze procurement data.
- Supplier relationship management (SRM) systems to track supplier performance and collaboration.
- E-procurement solutions for automating purchasing processes and ensuring compliance.
- Analytics and reporting tools to measure category performance and provide actionable insights.

The integration of these tools with existing enterprise resource planning (ERP) systems ensures seamless data sharing and process efficiency.

Roles and Responsibilities in Category Teams

Category Management requires the formation of dedicated category teams, composed of individuals with diverse skills and expertise. These teams are responsible for developing and executing category strategies, managing supplier relationships, and ensuring alignment with organizational objectives.

Key roles within a category team include:

Category Manager:
The Category Manager serves as the leader of the category team, overseeing all activities related to a specific category. Responsibilities include:

- Conducting spend analysis and market research.
- Developing and implementing category strategies.
- Managing supplier relationships and negotiations.
- Monitoring category performance and driving continuous improvement.

Procurement Analysts:
Procurement analysts support the category team by providing data-driven insights. Their responsibilities include:

- Conducting spend analysis and supplier performance evaluations.
- Identifying cost-saving opportunities and efficiency improvements.
- Supporting strategy development with market intelligence and trend analysis.

Supplier Relationship Managers:
This role focuses on fostering strong relationships with key suppliers. Responsibilities include:

- Monitoring supplier performance and addressing issues proactively.
- Facilitating collaboration on innovation and process improvements.
- Ensuring compliance with contractual obligations and service-level agreements.

Cross-Functional Stakeholders:
Category teams also include representatives from other business units, such as finance, operations, and marketing. These stakeholders provide input on category requirements, participate in strategy development, and ensure alignment with organizational goals.

Executive Sponsors:
Executive sponsors provide strategic oversight and ensure that Category Management initiatives receive adequate support and resources. They play a crucial role in removing barriers, resolving conflicts, and championing the program across the organization.

In conclusion, organizational readiness for Category Management depends on assessing current procurement maturity, building essential capabilities, and defining clear roles and responsibilities within category teams. By addressing these elements, organizations can create a strong foundation for Category Management, enabling them to achieve superior outcomes in cost efficiency, supplier collaboration, and value creation.

Chapter 4: Spend Analysis and Data Management

Importance of Spend Analysis in Category Management

Spend analysis is the cornerstone of effective category management. It involves the systematic collection, cleansing, categorization, and analysis of expenditure data to understand an organization's purchasing patterns and identify opportunities for improvement. This process provides the insights needed to make informed decisions, align procurement strategies with business goals, and drive significant cost savings and value creation.

In category management, the role of spend analysis extends beyond cost reduction. It enables organizations to achieve a deeper understanding of their supplier base, identify risks, and uncover inefficiencies in procurement processes. By analyzing historical spending data, procurement professionals can segment expenditures into meaningful categories, prioritize high-value opportunities, and establish baselines for measuring performance improvements.

One of the key benefits of spend analysis is its ability to provide visibility into organizational spending. In many organizations, spending is fragmented across departments, locations, or business units, leading to inefficiencies and missed opportunities for consolidation. Spend analysis addresses this challenge by providing a centralized view of all expenditures. This transparency allows organizations to identify patterns, such as excessive reliance on specific suppliers, inconsistent pricing, or non-compliance with procurement policies.

Spend analysis also supports strategic decision-making by revealing insights into supplier performance and market dynamics. For example, organizations can assess the reliability, quality, and cost-effectiveness of their suppliers by comparing their performance metrics against benchmarks. This information is invaluable for negotiating better terms, consolidating supplier bases, or diversifying sourcing strategies to reduce risk.

Furthermore, spend analysis plays a critical role in aligning procurement activities with organizational goals such as sustainability, risk mitigation, or innovation. By analyzing spending patterns, organizations can identify opportunities to source from sustainable suppliers, reduce dependency on high-risk regions, or engage suppliers that offer innovative solutions. This alignment ensures that category management contributes to broader strategic objectives, beyond just cost efficiency.

Tools and Techniques for Analyzing Spend Data

The effectiveness of spend analysis depends on the tools and techniques used to collect, process, and interpret data. In today's data-driven business environment, advanced tools and technologies enable procurement professionals to extract actionable insights from complex and voluminous data sets. These tools not only enhance the accuracy and efficiency of spend analysis but also empower organizations to make proactive, data-informed decisions.

Spend analysis typically begins with the collection of data from various sources, including enterprise resource planning (ERP) systems, procurement platforms, and financial systems. This data is then cleansed and standardized to ensure consistency and accuracy. Common challenges during this phase include duplicate records, inconsistent categorization, and incomplete data, all of which can skew analysis results. Advanced data cleansing tools can automate this process, reducing errors and saving time.

Once the data is prepared, it is categorized using classification frameworks such as the United Nations Standard Products and Services Code (UNSPSC) or the North American Industry Classification System (NAICS). These frameworks group expenditures into meaningful categories, enabling organizations to analyze spending patterns within specific areas. For example, expenditures on IT hardware, office supplies, or raw materials can be analyzed separately to identify trends and opportunities.

Analytical techniques such as Pareto analysis, regression analysis, and predictive modeling are commonly used to extract insights from spend data. Pareto analysis, also known as the 80/20 rule, helps organizations identify high-impact areas where a small percentage of suppliers or categories account for the majority of spending. Regression analysis can uncover correlations between variables, such as supplier pricing and order volumes, to optimize sourcing decisions. Predictive modeling leverages historical data to forecast future spending trends, enabling organizations to anticipate needs and negotiate favorable terms.

Visualization tools such as dashboards and reports play a crucial role in presenting spend analysis findings in an easily digestible format. Modern procurement platforms offer interactive dashboards that provide real-time insights into spending patterns, supplier performance, and category performance. These dashboards enable procurement teams to track key performance indicators (KPIs), identify anomalies, and drill down into specific categories for detailed analysis.

The integration of advanced technologies such as artificial intelligence (AI), machine learning, and big data analytics is transforming spend analysis. AI-powered tools can analyze vast amounts of data at unprecedented speeds, identify patterns that may be overlooked by human analysts, and provide recommendations for optimizing procurement strategies. Machine learning algorithms can continuously improve the accuracy of spend categorization and predictive models, ensuring that organizations stay ahead of market dynamics.

Identifying Opportunities from Data Insights

The ultimate goal of spend analysis is to uncover actionable opportunities that drive value for the organization. Data insights derived from spend analysis can reveal inefficiencies, risks, and strategic opportunities that would otherwise remain hidden. These insights empower procurement professionals to make decisions that improve cost efficiency, enhance supplier performance, and align procurement strategies with business objectives.

One of the most significant opportunities identified through spend analysis is cost savings. By consolidating purchases across categories or suppliers, organizations can leverage economies of scale to negotiate better pricing or terms. For instance, if spend analysis reveals that multiple business units are purchasing similar items from different suppliers, consolidating these purchases with a single supplier can result in significant cost reductions.

Spend analysis also identifies opportunities for process improvement. For example, analyzing purchasing patterns may reveal excessive reliance on spot buys or non-contracted suppliers, leading to higher costs and reduced compliance. Addressing these issues by increasing the use of preferred suppliers or automating routine purchases can streamline procurement processes and reduce costs.

Risk mitigation is another critical opportunity uncovered through spend analysis. By analyzing supplier concentration, geographic dependencies, or financial stability, organizations can identify high-risk areas within their supply chain. Diversifying the supplier base, sourcing from alternative regions, or engaging suppliers with stronger financial positions can reduce exposure to risks such as supply disruptions, geopolitical instability, or financial insolvency.

Spend analysis also supports innovation and value creation by identifying opportunities to engage with suppliers that offer differentiated capabilities or innovative solutions. For example, organizations may discover suppliers with advanced technologies, unique expertise, or sustainable practices that align with their strategic goals. Collaborating with such suppliers can drive innovation, improve product quality, or enhance sustainability outcomes.

Furthermore, spend analysis provides insights into category performance, enabling organizations to tailor their category strategies for maximum impact. For example, high-spend categories with fragmented supplier bases may benefit from consolidation, while categories with stable demand and predictable pricing may be ideal candidates for long-term contracts. By aligning category strategies with data-driven insights, organizations can achieve superior outcomes in terms of cost efficiency, risk management, and value creation.

In conclusion, spend analysis and data management are foundational to the strategic category management process. By leveraging advanced tools and techniques to analyze spend data, organizations gain the visibility and insights needed to make informed decisions, optimize procurement strategies, and drive long-term value creation. The ability to identify actionable opportunities from data insights sets leading organizations apart, enabling them to achieve a competitive advantage in an increasingly complex and dynamic business environment.

Chapter 5: Understanding Supply Markets

Conducting Supplier and Market Analysis

Understanding supply markets is a critical component of successful category management. Supplier and market analysis allow procurement teams to gain insights into the dynamics that affect sourcing decisions, supplier relationships, and overall procurement strategy. A comprehensive market analysis involves evaluating both the supplier landscape and the broader industry or market in which suppliers operate, including potential risks, opportunities, and market conditions that could impact supply chains.

A key objective of supplier and market analysis is to assess the supply landscape to identify reliable and capable suppliers that align with an organization's needs and goals. This process includes reviewing supplier performance, financial health, capacity, innovation capabilities, and sustainability practices. Furthermore, it involves understanding the economic, political, and competitive factors that influence supply chains, including market trends, supply and demand fluctuations, and global events that may affect the cost and availability of goods and services.

Supplier analysis goes beyond simply identifying potential suppliers. It also focuses on evaluating existing supplier relationships to ensure they are contributing value, meeting performance expectations, and aligning with broader business goals. A supplier performance assessment considers factors such as on-time delivery, quality consistency, pricing structures, and adherence to contractual obligations. Based on this analysis, procurement teams can decide whether to maintain, expand, or end supplier relationships.

Market analysis also involves evaluating the competitiveness of a specific category or product/service in the broader supply market. This requires a deep understanding of market conditions, including supply-demand dynamics, the competitive landscape, price trends, and any emerging shifts that could impact sourcing decisions. Conducting market research to understand the forces shaping the supply market provides valuable context for making strategic sourcing decisions and negotiating favorable contracts.

Additionally, evaluating supplier capabilities helps procurement professionals identify gaps in the organization's supply chain, leading to opportunities to introduce new suppliers, change suppliers, or leverage supplier development to improve performance. Recognizing weaknesses in the supplier base can help organizations build a more resilient and competitive procurement function.

Key Tools: Porter's Five Forces, SWOT, and PESTLE Analysis

Several analytical tools can help procurement professionals understand supply markets in-depth. These tools assist in evaluating market forces, competitive dynamics, and external factors that influence procurement decisions. Among the most widely used tools in supply market analysis are Porter's Five Forces, SWOT analysis, and PESTLE analysis.

Porter's Five Forces is a strategic tool developed by Michael Porter to assess the competitive forces within an industry. It evaluates the following five forces that shape competition and influence the attractiveness of a market:

> **Threat of New Entrants**: This force assesses the barriers to entry in a particular market. High barriers, such as significant capital investment, complex technology, or strict regulations, reduce the likelihood of new competitors entering the market and driving down profits for existing suppliers. Conversely, low barriers to entry increase competition, which may impact the pricing and availability of goods or services.

Bargaining Power of Suppliers: This force evaluates how much power suppliers have in influencing prices and terms. If suppliers are few or have unique offerings, their bargaining power increases, allowing them to set higher prices or impose unfavorable terms. On the other hand, a larger number of suppliers or substitute products reduces their power.

Bargaining Power of Buyers: This force looks at how much influence buyers (in this case, the organization) have over suppliers. In markets where buyers can easily switch suppliers or when they represent large volumes of demand, they possess greater bargaining power, which can be leveraged to negotiate better prices or terms.

Threat of Substitutes: This force considers the potential for alternative products or services to replace what is currently being supplied. If there are many substitutes available or if technological innovations could lead to alternatives, suppliers may be forced to lower prices or innovate to remain competitive.

Industry Rivalry: This force assesses the level of competition within the market. High rivalry among existing suppliers can lead to price wars, reduced margins, and a focus on differentiation. When competition is low, suppliers may have more room to set prices and terms to their advantage.

By understanding these forces, procurement teams can make better decisions regarding supplier selection, contract negotiations, and risk management. It provides insight into market trends, supplier power, and the overall competitive environment, which helps organizations position themselves strategically within their supply market.

SWOT Analysis is another key tool in understanding supply markets and suppliers. SWOT analysis evaluates a supplier's internal strengths and weaknesses, as well as the external opportunities and threats they face in the marketplace.

Strengths: This refers to the advantages a supplier possesses, such as cost leadership, innovation capabilities, robust supply chains, or a strong brand reputation. Understanding supplier strengths helps procurement teams assess which suppliers are best positioned to deliver value to the organization.

Weaknesses: This refers to the internal challenges faced by a supplier, such as poor financial health, inadequate infrastructure, or a lack of skilled labor. Identifying weaknesses allows procurement professionals to manage risks and evaluate whether it's worth investing in supplier development to address these challenges.

Opportunities: External factors such as new technologies, emerging markets, or regulatory changes may present opportunities for suppliers to innovate or expand their offerings. Understanding these opportunities enables organizations to align their category strategies with future trends and growth areas.

Threats: This refers to external factors such as economic downturns, political instability, supply chain disruptions, or increased competition that could negatively impact a supplier's performance. Identifying potential threats allows organizations to take proactive measures to mitigate risks and secure alternative sources of supply.

Lastly, **PESTLE Analysis** (Political, Economic, Social, Technological, Legal, and Environmental) is a tool that helps organizations assess the broader macroeconomic and socio-political factors affecting the supply market.

Political: Examining political factors helps organizations understand the impact of government policies, regulations, tariffs, and trade agreements on the supply chain. Political instability in certain regions or countries can pose significant risks to procurement activities.

Economic: Economic factors such as inflation, exchange rates, and labor costs influence supplier pricing, availability of raw materials, and demand for products or services. Economic conditions must be closely monitored to ensure sourcing strategies align with market realities.

Social: Social factors refer to consumer trends, cultural preferences, and demographic shifts. For example, the increasing demand for sustainable or ethically sourced products may influence supply market dynamics, requiring procurement teams to identify suppliers with responsible practices.

Technological: Technological advancements can disrupt supply markets, leading to new production methods, materials, or sourcing strategies. Staying updated on technological trends can help procurement teams stay ahead of innovations that improve efficiency or reduce costs.

Legal: Legal factors, such as changes in labor laws, environmental regulations, or trade restrictions, can have a significant impact on supply markets. Procurement professionals must remain compliant with all applicable laws to minimize risk.

Environmental: Environmental considerations such as climate change, resource scarcity, and sustainability initiatives are becoming increasingly important in supply markets. Understanding environmental trends allows procurement professionals to make more responsible and future-proof sourcing decisions.

Identifying Market Trends and Supply Chain Risks

The final component of supply market analysis is identifying market trends and potential supply chain risks. These trends can include shifts in consumer behavior, technological advancements, changes in global trade policies, or fluctuations in supply and demand. Identifying trends allows organizations to anticipate changes in the market and adjust their category strategies accordingly. For example, procurement teams might identify a growing demand for green or sustainable products, prompting them to source from suppliers with eco-friendly practices.

Similarly, identifying potential supply chain risks is a critical aspect of supplier and market analysis. Risks can arise from various sources, such as geopolitical instability, natural disasters, cybersecurity threats, or supply disruptions. Risk mitigation strategies might include diversifying the supplier base, creating contingency plans, or securing alternative sources of critical goods.

In conclusion, understanding supply markets is an essential part of effective category management. Through supplier and market analysis, organizations can gain insights into the competitive forces, risks, and trends that shape procurement decisions. By leveraging tools such as Porter's Five Forces, SWOT, and PESTLE analysis, procurement teams can identify opportunities, mitigate risks, and develop more robust sourcing strategies that drive value for the organization.

Chapter 6: Segmenting Categories for Maximum Value

Category Segmentation and Prioritization

Category segmentation is a fundamental practice in category management, helping organizations maximize value by grouping and prioritizing categories based on various factors. By understanding the distinct characteristics of different procurement categories, companies can tailor their strategies to each segment, aligning their approach to the specific value they want to achieve.

Segmentation involves categorizing products or services into groups with similar traits or requirements, such as the complexity of sourcing, spend volume, risk factors, and strategic importance to the organization. This approach enables procurement teams to develop targeted strategies that maximize the value of each category, rather than adopting a one-size-fits-all model.

The first step in category segmentation is to assess the spend and risk factors associated with each category. Spend analysis provides an understanding of the overall expenditure within each category, helping procurement teams identify which categories contribute the most to the total procurement budget. High-spend categories often require more attention and strategic sourcing, while low-spend categories may be managed more efficiently with simplified processes.

Risk analysis, on the other hand, considers factors like supplier dependency, supply chain volatility, and geopolitical risks that could impact the availability or cost of goods and services. High-risk categories might warrant more careful supplier management and alternative sourcing strategies, while lower-risk categories can often be managed with more standard procurement practices.

Once categories are segmented based on spend and risk, the next step is prioritizing them. Prioritization involves ranking categories according to their strategic importance to the organization. High-priority categories—those that are critical to the company's core operations or competitive advantage—require more strategic attention, complex supplier relationships, and higher levels of investment. Conversely, lower-priority categories might be outsourced to third-party vendors or managed with less direct oversight.

By segmenting categories in this manner, organizations can allocate their resources efficiently, ensuring that the most critical categories receive the attention they deserve, while low-impact categories are managed with less effort. This strategic alignment between procurement activities and organizational goals ultimately leads to better value generation and improved supplier relationships.

Kraljic Matrix and Strategic Sourcing Models

The Kraljic Matrix is a well-established tool used to categorize procurement items based on two critical factors: **supply risk** and **profit impact**. The matrix helps organizations prioritize procurement efforts by identifying which categories require a more strategic approach and which can be managed more tactically. The four quadrants of the Kraljic Matrix—non-critical items, leverage items, bottleneck items, and strategic items—represent different categories of procurement based on their level of importance and associated risks.

> **Non-Critical Items**: These categories typically involve low-cost items with low supply risk. The procurement process for these categories is straightforward and often managed through simplified purchasing methods. For example, office supplies or low-cost, easily sourced commodities might fall into

this category. The focus here is on operational efficiency and cost control, with minimal supplier interaction.

Leverage Items: These items have a high profit impact but low supply risk. These categories are strategically important but can be sourced from multiple suppliers, providing procurement teams with negotiation leverage. Examples include common raw materials or standardized components that are critical to the production process but are readily available from multiple sources. The primary strategy for these categories is cost reduction, and procurement teams often engage in competitive bidding to obtain the best prices.

Bottleneck Items: Bottleneck items represent a high supply risk but a low profit impact. These are often specialized or niche products or services that are critical to operations but may be sourced from limited suppliers. The procurement team's focus for these categories is risk mitigation, ensuring supply continuity, and finding alternative sources if necessary. For example, a specialized piece of equipment or rare material with only one or two suppliers might be considered a bottleneck item. Strong supplier relationship management and careful inventory planning are essential to mitigate risks associated with bottleneck items.

Strategic Items: Strategic items are both high in supply risk and high in profit impact. These categories are critical to the success of the organization and typically involve long-term contracts or deep supplier partnerships. Strategic items could include key components of a product, critical technology, or exclusive raw materials. Given their high importance and risk, these items require a proactive and collaborative approach with suppliers, focusing on building strong, mutually beneficial relationships, joint innovation, and long-term planning.

The Kraljic Matrix helps procurement professionals develop tailored strategies for managing each category based on its unique characteristics. By recognizing the varying levels of risk and profit impact, organizations can prioritize resources, mitigate risks, and negotiate effectively to achieve maximum value.

Another strategic sourcing model commonly used in category management is the **Strategic Sourcing Process**. This process emphasizes a structured approach to supplier selection and relationship management. It involves a series of steps, including market research, supplier evaluation, and performance monitoring, with a focus on creating long-term value through strategic partnerships. The strategic sourcing process aligns procurement activities with business objectives, ensuring that suppliers are selected based not only on cost considerations but also on their ability to meet quality, delivery, and innovation requirements.

Tailoring Strategies for Different Categories

Not all procurement categories are created equal, and therefore, procurement strategies must be tailored to fit the specific characteristics of each category. Tailoring strategies based on category segmentation is essential for achieving maximum value, reducing risk, and optimizing procurement outcomes.

For **non-critical items**, the strategy focuses on efficiency and simplicity. These items often benefit from automated purchasing systems or online procurement tools, which allow the organization to streamline purchasing processes and reduce administrative overhead. By leveraging bulk purchasing or supplier consolidation, organizations can negotiate lower prices without significant effort. These items require minimal supplier engagement and limited management attention, allowing procurement teams to focus on more strategic categories.

For **leverage items**, the focus shifts to negotiation and cost reduction. Procurement teams should take advantage of the competitive market environment for these items, using techniques like volume-based pricing, long-term contracts, or tender processes to secure the best deals. Strong supplier relationships are important, but the focus remains on obtaining the best possible price for the organization. By strategically consolidating demand across categories, organizations can achieve economies of scale, further driving down costs.

In the case of **bottleneck items**, procurement strategies should prioritize risk management and security of supply. These items may require more time and attention, as the supply base is often limited or constrained. Organizations may need to invest in building strong relationships with existing suppliers, negotiating favorable terms, and exploring alternative suppliers to mitigate potential disruptions. In some cases, businesses might consider vertical integration or diversification of their supplier base to reduce dependency on a single source. Furthermore, strategic inventory management and long-term contracts may help ensure supply stability for bottleneck items.

Finally, for **strategic items**, procurement strategies should focus on long-term value creation, supplier collaboration, and risk sharing. Given the critical importance of these items, procurement teams should work closely with suppliers to innovate, improve product quality, and optimize the supply chain. Strategic sourcing models, such as supplier development programs or joint ventures, can be employed to create mutually beneficial partnerships. These categories often require extensive market research, supplier capability assessments, and performance monitoring to ensure that both parties are aligned with long-term business objectives.

In conclusion, segmenting categories for maximum value is an essential practice in category management, helping organizations prioritize their procurement efforts and allocate resources effectively. The Kraljic Matrix provides a valuable framework for understanding the strategic importance and risks associated with different categories, while tailoring strategies to fit each category's specific needs allows procurement teams to drive value, reduce risks, and achieve organizational goals. By understanding the unique characteristics of each category, organizations can build a more effective, resilient, and cost-efficient procurement function.

Chapter 7: Developing Category Strategies

Defining Objectives and Goals for Each Category

The development of effective category strategies begins with a clear understanding of the objectives and goals for each category. These objectives serve as the foundation for all subsequent actions and decisions, guiding procurement teams in their efforts to create value through strategic sourcing. To define these objectives, it is essential to consider the unique characteristics of each category, such as its importance to the business, the level of supply risk, and the potential for cost savings.

Each category should have specific, measurable, achievable, relevant, and time-bound (SMART) objectives that align with the broader procurement and organizational goals. These objectives can vary significantly depending on the nature of the category. For instance, the objective for a **strategic category** might be to ensure uninterrupted supply and foster supplier innovation, while for a **leverage category**, the primary goal could be to secure cost savings through negotiation and volume consolidation.

One of the first steps in defining category objectives is understanding the role that each category plays within the organization. A category that provides critical components for manufacturing or research and development will have objectives focused on ensuring continuity of supply, optimizing quality, and securing supplier collaboration. Conversely, categories that consist of non-critical or commodity items might have objectives centered around cost reduction, streamlining procurement processes, and ensuring efficiency.

It is also important to incorporate stakeholder inputs when defining category objectives. These stakeholders may include internal departments such as finance, operations, and R&D, as well as external partners like suppliers and customers.

Engaging these stakeholders ensures that the category objectives are aligned with the needs of the broader organization and that procurement strategies support corporate goals.

For example, in a manufacturing context, a category that supplies essential raw materials may have the objective of achieving price stability and minimizing disruptions in the supply chain. For an IT-related category, the objective could focus on maintaining cutting-edge technology while ensuring competitive pricing and strong vendor support. The flexibility and adaptability of these objectives are crucial, as they must evolve in response to changing business environments and market conditions.

Aligning Strategies with Organizational Goals

Once category objectives are defined, the next crucial step is to align them with the broader organizational goals. This alignment ensures that procurement activities not only meet the needs of individual categories but also contribute to the overarching objectives of the business. The alignment between category strategies and corporate goals is vital for ensuring that procurement decisions support the long-term strategic direction of the company.

At the corporate level, goals may include growth, profitability, sustainability, or market leadership. For procurement, this means developing strategies that support these goals while considering the specific requirements of each category. For example, if an organization's primary goal is to expand into new markets, procurement strategies for categories that support product development or logistics could focus on ensuring cost-effective and reliable sourcing of critical materials and components that support expansion efforts.

Similarly, if the organization is focused on sustainability, the procurement team might prioritize suppliers who demonstrate strong environmental practices, use sustainable materials, or engage in fair labor practices. Aligning category strategies with sustainability goals would mean that procurement teams engage with suppliers that share the company's commitment to reducing environmental impacts, even if this comes at a slightly higher cost.

In many cases, procurement is expected to contribute to the organization's profitability by securing competitive pricing, improving supplier relationships, and ensuring operational efficiency. However, this cost-focus should be balanced with a recognition that, in some cases, higher investments in quality or long-term supplier partnerships may be necessary to support strategic business objectives. For instance, a company seeking to innovate its product line might prioritize quality and supplier collaboration over cost savings to ensure that the highest standards of product development are met.

Aligning procurement strategies with organizational goals requires close collaboration with other departments. Procurement teams need to be involved early in the strategic planning process, ensuring that category strategies are integrated into the business's broader vision. Moreover, cross-functional teams should be established to ensure that procurement aligns its priorities with the objectives of R&D, marketing, operations, and finance. This collaboration ensures that procurement contributes to the business's success in a meaningful way.

Balancing Cost, Quality, and Risk

One of the central challenges of developing category strategies is finding the right balance between cost, quality, and risk.

These three elements are often in tension with each other, and achieving the right equilibrium is crucial to maximizing value while minimizing potential issues.

Cost: Cost is a critical factor for most organizations, and procurement teams are often tasked with finding ways to reduce expenses and improve the bottom line. However, focusing solely on cost reduction can lead to suboptimal decisions, such as compromising on quality or accepting increased risk. For example, selecting the lowest-cost supplier might result in lower quality or unreliable delivery, ultimately leading to higher long-term costs.

Quality: Quality is another crucial factor that must be carefully considered in category strategies. High-quality products or services ensure customer satisfaction, minimize defects, and reduce the risk of costly rework or replacements. In some categories, particularly those tied to core business functions, quality may take precedence over cost. However, consistently prioritizing quality over cost can strain budgets, especially when dealing with high-spend categories. A procurement strategy focused solely on quality could result in excessive investments in high-end suppliers or products that exceed what is necessary to meet organizational needs.

Risk: Risk management is equally essential, particularly when dealing with categories that are critical to operations or have high supply chain dependencies. Risk factors can include market volatility, geopolitical uncertainty, supplier reliability, and changes in regulation. Procurement strategies must be designed to mitigate these risks, which could involve working with multiple suppliers, diversifying sources, negotiating long-term contracts, or investing in technology for enhanced supply chain visibility.

The key challenge is balancing these three elements. For example, a category strategy for a critical component may involve paying a premium for higher-quality suppliers to ensure reliability and mitigate the risk of supply disruptions. Alternatively, a less critical category might focus on cost reduction, using competitive bidding to drive down expenses without compromising quality or increasing risk. Risk mitigation measures—such as diversifying the supplier base or engaging in supplier development programs—can help balance quality and cost considerations without exposing the organization to undue risks.

Ultimately, the balance between cost, quality, and risk must be determined by the strategic importance of the category, the overall business objectives, and the risk tolerance of the organization. Procurement teams must carefully assess each category's unique characteristics and define strategies that align with both the immediate needs of the business and its long-term goals. This requires a deep understanding of the market, supplier capabilities, and the broader business environment.

Effective category strategies often include mechanisms to measure and track the performance of these elements. Key performance indicators (KPIs) such as total cost of ownership (TCO), supplier performance metrics, quality control indicators, and risk assessments can help procurement teams monitor whether they are achieving the desired balance and making progress toward their strategic goals.

In conclusion, developing category strategies requires a thoughtful and strategic approach that balances the often competing demands of cost, quality, and risk. By defining clear objectives, aligning strategies with organizational goals, and carefully managing these key factors, procurement teams can create category strategies that deliver maximum value and contribute to the overall success of the business.

8. Supplier Relationship Management (SRM)

Supplier Relationship Management (SRM) is a cornerstone of effective category management, emphasizing the importance of fostering strategic and collaborative relationships with key suppliers. By transitioning from a transactional procurement model to a partnership-based approach, organizations can unlock significant value through innovation, cost optimization, and improved supply chain resilience. This chapter delves into the principles of SRM, the methodologies for building and sustaining effective supplier relationships, and the tools that facilitate these efforts.

Building Strategic Relationships with Key Suppliers

Strategic relationships with suppliers extend beyond the traditional buyer-supplier dynamic. In a competitive and interconnected global marketplace, suppliers are increasingly seen as partners who can contribute to an organization's strategic goals. Building such relationships requires a structured approach:

1. Understanding Supplier Importance

Not all suppliers are equal in terms of their impact on organizational success. Strategic relationships are typically established with suppliers who provide critical goods or services, possess unique capabilities, or represent a significant spend category. The Kraljic Matrix is a helpful tool in identifying such suppliers by evaluating factors like supply risk and business impact.

2. Establishing Trust and Transparency

Trust forms the foundation of any successful supplier relationship. Clear communication, transparent dealings, and mutual respect are essential to fostering a culture of collaboration. Regular engagement and open discussions about challenges and opportunities can enhance mutual trust.

3. Aligning Objectives and Goals
Alignment of organizational and supplier objectives ensures both parties are working toward common outcomes. This involves sharing long-term strategies, key performance indicators (KPIs), and expectations. Strategic alignment helps avoid conflicts and promotes cohesive efforts in achieving mutual success.

4. Investing in Supplier Development
Organizations often invest in developing the capabilities of strategic suppliers. This could include technical training, joint innovation projects, or providing access to market insights. Such investments strengthen the supplier's ability to meet the organization's evolving needs.

Collaborative vs. Transactional Approaches

Procurement relationships can generally be categorized into collaborative and transactional approaches, each with distinct characteristics, benefits, and applications.

Collaborative Approach
The collaborative model is built on long-term partnerships and mutual value creation. Key features include joint problem-solving, shared risks and rewards, and proactive engagement in innovation. Collaborative relationships are particularly valuable for strategic suppliers who are critical to achieving competitive advantages.

Advantages:

- Enhanced innovation through joint efforts
- Greater flexibility in adapting to market changes
- Stronger supply chain resilience and risk management

Challenges:

- Requires higher levels of investment in time and resources
- Potential for conflicts if objectives are misaligned

Transactional Approach
The transactional model focuses on short-term, cost-driven interactions. It is often applied to non-critical or commoditized categories where supplier differentiation is minimal. The primary goal is achieving cost efficiency and ensuring supply continuity.

Advantages:

- Simplicity and ease of implementation
- Low overhead costs in relationship management

Challenges:

- Limited scope for innovation and value addition
- Higher risk of supply disruptions in volatile markets

Tools for SRM: Scorecards, Dashboards, and Relationship Mapping

Effective SRM relies on robust tools and methodologies to evaluate and enhance supplier relationships. These tools provide data-driven insights and facilitate informed decision-making.

Supplier Scorecards
Scorecards are structured tools used to evaluate supplier performance against predefined KPIs. These KPIs often cover aspects such as delivery reliability, quality standards, cost efficiency, and innovation contributions. Regular scoring helps

identify performance gaps and fosters a culture of continuous improvement.

Key Components of Supplier Scorecards:

- Quantitative metrics (e.g., on-time delivery percentages, defect rates)
- Qualitative assessments (e.g., responsiveness, adaptability)
- Weighting systems to prioritize critical performance areas

Supplier Dashboards
Dashboards offer a real-time, visual representation of supplier performance metrics. By integrating data from multiple sources, dashboards provide a comprehensive view of supplier activities and their impact on the organization. Advanced dashboards may leverage analytics and predictive modeling to forecast future performance trends.

Benefits of Dashboards:

- Enhanced visibility into supplier operations
- Early identification of potential issues
- Support for strategic decision-making

Relationship Mapping
Relationship mapping involves visualizing the interconnectedness of stakeholders within the supplier network and the organization. It highlights the key points of interaction, areas of influence, and potential bottlenecks in collaboration.

Applications of Relationship Mapping:

- Identifying decision-makers and influencers on both sides
- Clarifying roles and responsibilities
- Enhancing communication flow and resolving conflicts

Integrating SRM into Organizational Processes

For SRM to be effective, it must be integrated into the broader category management framework and aligned with organizational objectives. This involves cross-functional collaboration, leveraging technology, and embedding SRM principles into corporate culture.

Cross-Functional Collaboration
SRM thrives on input from diverse functions such as procurement, operations, finance, and quality assurance. Cross-functional teams ensure that supplier strategies align with overall business goals and reflect diverse organizational needs.

Technology Enablement
Modern SRM relies heavily on digital tools such as Supplier Relationship Management software, e-procurement platforms, and AI-driven analytics. These tools streamline processes, enhance data accuracy, and facilitate deeper insights into supplier dynamics.

Cultural Embedding
Finally, SRM should become a core component of the organization's procurement philosophy. Leadership support, regular training programs, and recognition of supplier collaboration successes can foster a culture that prioritizes strategic supplier relationships.

Supplier Relationship Management represents a paradigm shift in how organizations engage with their suppliers. By focusing on strategic alignment, collaboration, and leveraging advanced tools, SRM not only enhances procurement outcomes but also builds resilient, value-driven supply chains capable of navigating the complexities of today's global markets.

Chapter 9: Procurement and Negotiation Strategies

Advanced Negotiation Techniques for Category Managers

Effective negotiation is one of the most critical skills in category management. As category managers engage with suppliers to secure favorable terms, they must employ advanced negotiation techniques to ensure that both short-term goals and long-term strategic objectives are met. Mastering these techniques can lead to significant cost savings, improved supplier relationships, and better risk management.

One advanced technique involves the **"principled negotiation" approach**, which focuses on mutual gains rather than a win-lose outcome. Popularized by Roger Fisher and William Ury in their book *Getting to Yes*, this approach encourages negotiators to separate the people from the problem, focus on interests rather than positions, and generate options for mutual benefit. By emphasizing collaboration, category managers can often secure terms that are favorable to both parties while building stronger, long-lasting relationships with suppliers.

Another important negotiation tactic is **"anchoring,"** where the negotiator sets the initial offer or frame of reference. This technique establishes the starting point for discussions, shaping the range of possible outcomes. For instance, by anchoring price expectations in the early stages of negotiations, category managers can influence the final outcome by directing the supplier's concession space toward more favorable terms for their organization.

BATNA (Best Alternative to a Negotiated Agreement) is a crucial tool for category managers. Having a strong BATNA provides leverage during negotiations by ensuring that the manager is not overly dependent on one supplier or solution. Understanding alternatives allows category managers to remain confident and avoid making concessions that undermine the organization's position. A clear BATNA can also guide decisions when negotiations reach an impasse or when suppliers are not meeting desired terms.

Moreover, effective category managers use **"win-win" strategies** that seek to benefit both parties involved. For instance, exploring non-price-related value, such as improved delivery terms, service guarantees, or longer contract durations, can result in a favorable agreement without reducing price expectations. Additionally, creating an environment of transparency during negotiations fosters trust and collaboration, which can lead to more favorable long-term partnerships.

One tactic that has proven effective in some industries is **"multi-party negotiation,"** where category managers engage with several suppliers simultaneously. This can create a competitive atmosphere that drives suppliers to offer better terms, knowing that other competitors are bidding for the same category. This approach also enhances the leverage of the category manager as they can use competitive offers to pressure suppliers into improving their proposals.

Advanced negotiation techniques are not only about extracting the best deal, but also about building relationships with suppliers. These relationships are fundamental to category management success, as collaboration and communication play a significant role in securing mutually beneficial outcomes. Category managers must always consider the long-term view, understanding that good negotiations today can pave the way for smoother engagements and more favorable terms in future deals.

Total Cost of Ownership (TCO) vs. Price Focus

A common pitfall in traditional procurement is a narrow focus on **price** as the primary metric for supplier selection. While price is undoubtedly important, focusing solely on it often neglects other critical factors that contribute to the overall value of a purchase. This is where the concept of **Total Cost of Ownership (TCO)** comes into play, offering a more holistic approach to procurement decisions.

TCO refers to the comprehensive cost associated with the acquisition, use, and disposal of a product or service. This includes not only the initial purchase price, but also the **operational costs**, such as maintenance, repair, training, and energy consumption. Additionally, TCO accounts for costs related to downtime, warranty claims, and the eventual disposal or recycling of the product. By considering TCO, category managers can evaluate the full lifecycle cost of a product or service, rather than simply focusing on the upfront price.

For instance, when procuring machinery or equipment, the initial cost might seem attractive, but if the equipment requires frequent repairs, consumes excessive energy, or has a short lifespan, the total cost of ownership could far exceed that of a higher-priced but more efficient alternative. Similarly, when purchasing software or IT services, there might be ongoing licensing fees, implementation costs, and training expenses that should be factored into the overall cost equation.

Using TCO as a basis for procurement decisions aligns with the broader strategic goals of category management. It supports the idea of **long-term value optimization**, ensuring that procurement decisions are not based solely on short-term price savings. By integrating TCO into their decision-making process, category managers are better positioned to make informed choices that optimize total value, reduce risks, and improve supplier performance over the long term.

However, it's important to note that TCO analysis is not a one-size-fits-all solution. For certain categories, price may still be the dominant factor. In highly competitive, low-margin markets, for example, a focus on price might be necessary. But even in these cases, TCO can be used to identify hidden costs that might arise over time and inform better contract terms.

To incorporate TCO effectively, category managers must ensure they have access to reliable data on all relevant cost factors. This includes not only direct costs but also indirect costs associated with product or service usage. In addition, the procurement team must be skilled in modeling TCO over the expected life cycle of the product or service, accounting for fluctuations in costs and potential risks that may arise.

Using TCO in procurement requires a mindset shift. It requires category managers to look beyond the immediate cost and consider the total value delivered by the supplier. This approach fosters more strategic, informed decision-making and ensures that procurement decisions align with broader organizational goals, such as profitability, sustainability, and efficiency.

Managing Contract Lifecycles

Once a procurement negotiation has resulted in a signed agreement, category managers must focus on the next crucial aspect: managing the **contract lifecycle**. The contract lifecycle is a key component of procurement that spans the entire duration of the relationship between the buyer and the supplier. It encompasses the negotiation, execution, performance monitoring, and eventual renewal or termination of the contract.

The management of the contract lifecycle begins during the **contract negotiation** phase. Category managers must ensure that the terms of the contract reflect the organization's strategic goals and protect its interests. This involves drafting clear, concise, and comprehensive terms that address price, quality standards, delivery schedules, payment terms, dispute resolution mechanisms, and other critical elements. Moreover, it's essential to include provisions for monitoring supplier performance and ensuring compliance with agreed-upon terms.

One of the key challenges in managing the contract lifecycle is ensuring **performance management**. Effective contract management involves monitoring supplier performance against the agreed-upon terms, ensuring that deliverables are met on time and within quality standards. It's vital for category managers to establish clear performance metrics and KPIs that align with the contract's objectives. These metrics should be reviewed periodically to ensure that suppliers are fulfilling their obligations and delivering value.

Another important aspect of contract lifecycle management is **change management**. Over the course of a contract, circumstances may change, such as fluctuations in demand, changes in market conditions, or evolving business requirements. Category managers must be prepared to manage changes to the contract, whether that involves renegotiating terms, updating deliverables, or modifying the scope of the agreement. Effective change management requires flexibility, clear communication, and a collaborative approach with the supplier to ensure that both parties are aligned and that any adjustments to the contract are mutually beneficial.

As contracts approach their expiration date, category managers must begin the **contract renewal** process. This includes evaluating the current supplier's performance, determining whether the supplier relationship continues to align with organizational goals, and deciding whether to renew, renegotiate, or seek alternative suppliers. If the decision is to continue the relationship, category managers should aim to build on the success of the previous contract, incorporating lessons learned and optimizing terms for the future.

In some cases, the contract may need to be terminated early, either due to underperformance, changes in business requirements, or external factors. In these situations, category managers must manage the **exit strategy** carefully to ensure a smooth transition. This may involve renegotiating terms or finding new suppliers while minimizing the disruption to the organization's operations.

Managing the entire contract lifecycle requires strong project management skills, an in-depth understanding of legal and compliance requirements, and the ability to foster ongoing collaboration with suppliers. A robust contract management system, supported by digital tools and technology, can help streamline this process by automating routine tasks, tracking key milestones, and providing visibility into supplier performance.

Ultimately, successful contract lifecycle management is about ensuring that the organization continues to derive maximum value from its supplier relationships while maintaining compliance with contractual terms and safeguarding against risks. Effective management of the contract lifecycle is an essential part of category management, ensuring that procurement strategies are successfully executed and that both short-term and long-term objectives are met.

Chapter 10: Implementing Category Plans

Transitioning from Strategy to Execution

Successfully transitioning from strategy to execution is often one of the most challenging aspects of category management. While developing a comprehensive category strategy is essential, ensuring that it is effectively executed requires careful planning, clear communication, and a coordinated approach across multiple teams and stakeholders. Category managers must translate strategic goals into actionable plans that are aligned with organizational priorities and objectives, ensuring that execution delivers tangible results.

The first step in this transition is to ensure that the category strategy is **clear, well-defined, and feasible**. This involves taking a deep dive into the strategy to understand the specific actions that need to be taken. Key elements such as cost reduction targets, supplier selection criteria, risk mitigation measures, and performance metrics must be clearly articulated. Once the strategy has been detailed, it's important to break it down into smaller, more manageable tasks that can be assigned to relevant teams or individuals. This process may involve setting specific deliverables, timelines, and resources needed for each task, which provides a roadmap for execution.

Another critical aspect of transitioning from strategy to execution is ensuring that the **organizational structure is aligned with the strategy**. Category managers need to ensure that the right people with the necessary skills are in place to carry out the tasks defined in the strategy. This may involve collaborating with internal departments like procurement, finance, legal, and operations, as well as engaging with external stakeholders such as suppliers and consultants. It's important that these stakeholders are not only informed about the category strategy but are also aligned on the strategic objectives and goals.

A key tool in this transition is the **detailed action plan**, which provides a step-by-step guide for executing the category strategy. The action plan should include clear timelines, resource allocations, and defined roles and responsibilities. It should also outline key performance indicators (KPIs) and metrics that will be used to measure success at various stages. The action plan serves as a benchmark for performance and ensures that everyone involved in the execution process is working toward the same goals.

To facilitate a smooth transition, category managers must also focus on ensuring **organizational readiness** for execution. This may involve training and development, establishing processes and systems that support the strategy, and removing any barriers to successful implementation. By fostering a culture that embraces category management, the organization is more likely to execute the strategy effectively and meet the desired outcomes.

Effective Communication and Stakeholder Alignment

One of the most critical success factors in implementing category plans is ensuring **effective communication** with all stakeholders. Communication is not just about disseminating information; it's about ensuring that everyone involved understands their roles and responsibilities, the strategy's objectives, and how their actions contribute to the overall success of the category management process.

Effective communication begins with a **clear vision and a consistent message**. Category managers must ensure that all stakeholders, from internal teams to suppliers, understand the strategic objectives and how their contributions support these goals. This requires regular updates, feedback sessions, and open lines of communication. Stakeholders need to be informed of any changes in strategy, timelines, or expectations, ensuring that they are aligned at every stage of the execution process.

Stakeholder alignment is equally critical. Category managers must engage key stakeholders early in the process and maintain continuous dialogue throughout the implementation phase. This involves understanding the needs and concerns of different stakeholders, from procurement teams to senior executives, and ensuring that their objectives are aligned with the overall category strategy. One way to achieve this alignment is by creating a **stakeholder map** that identifies all relevant parties, their roles, and their level of involvement in the category plan's execution. This map can then be used to prioritize communication efforts and ensure that all stakeholders are kept informed at the appropriate times.

Moreover, **cross-functional collaboration** is often necessary for successful category plan implementation. Category managers need to work closely with departments such as finance, marketing, IT, and legal to ensure that the category strategy is integrated across the organization. Each department may have its own goals, challenges, and requirements, and it is essential to address these in the context of the category plan to ensure smooth execution. For example, finance may need to adjust budget allocations, while IT may need to support technology integration efforts, and legal teams may need to review contract terms. Effective communication ensures that all departments understand their roles in the larger category management strategy and work together to achieve the desired outcomes.

Transparent and consistent **reporting** is another key element of communication during the implementation phase. Regular status reports, progress updates, and milestone tracking ensure that everyone involved is aware of how the category plan is progressing. This not only helps to identify potential issues early on but also allows for adjustments to be made if necessary. Effective communication ensures that the strategy stays on track and that all stakeholders are working together toward a common goal.

Tracking Milestones and Deliverables

Tracking milestones and deliverables is a vital part of executing category plans effectively. Without proper monitoring, there is no way to determine if the strategy is on course, if adjustments are necessary, or if the goals are being achieved. Category managers must establish clear milestones and deliverables that serve as indicators of progress throughout the execution process.

Milestones are key points in the category management process that mark significant achievements or decision points. These could include completing the market analysis, selecting suppliers, finalizing contracts, or achieving specific cost-saving targets. By defining and tracking these milestones, category managers can ensure that the execution process is progressing as planned and that no critical tasks are missed. Additionally, milestones help to break down the execution process into manageable segments, making it easier to assess progress at each stage.

Deliverables, on the other hand, refer to the specific outputs or outcomes that must be achieved at various points throughout the execution phase. These could include deliverables such as final supplier contracts, procurement documents, performance reviews, or cost savings reports. Category managers should clearly define these deliverables at the outset of the execution process and ensure that they are measurable and achievable within the set timelines.

The use of **project management tools** can greatly assist in tracking milestones and deliverables. Tools such as Gantt charts, project management software, or performance dashboards provide a visual representation of the timeline and the progress made toward achieving milestones. These tools allow category managers to track performance in real time, identify bottlenecks or delays, and take corrective action if necessary. Real-time tracking also helps to keep stakeholders informed about the status of the category plan, ensuring that everyone remains aligned and focused on the tasks at hand.

In addition to tools, regular **review meetings** with key stakeholders are essential for tracking progress. These meetings provide an opportunity to evaluate progress, identify challenges, and make any necessary adjustments to the plan. Category managers should establish a routine for these meetings, whether weekly, bi-weekly, or monthly, depending on the complexity and duration of the implementation process. The review meetings should focus on assessing the completion of milestones and deliverables, discussing any potential risks or issues, and ensuring that the category plan stays on track.

Another important aspect of tracking milestones and deliverables is **performance measurement**. Category managers should have a clear set of key performance indicators (KPIs) in place that measure the success of the implementation process. These KPIs may include cost savings, supplier performance, contract compliance, and process efficiency. By regularly reviewing these KPIs, category managers can evaluate the effectiveness of the category plan and make any necessary adjustments to optimize performance.

Finally, tracking milestones and deliverables should also include **risk management**. As category plans are implemented, unforeseen challenges and risks may arise. Category managers must remain agile and proactive, using their tracking systems to identify potential risks early and develop mitigation strategies. Risk management ensures that the category plan remains adaptable and resilient, even in the face of external or internal challenges.

In conclusion, implementing category plans requires careful coordination, communication, and tracking to ensure success. Transitioning from strategy to execution, aligning stakeholders, and monitoring progress through milestones and deliverables are all critical components of the execution process. By effectively managing these elements, category managers can ensure that the strategic goals of the category management plan are achieved, delivering maximum value to the organization.

Chapter 11: Measuring and Managing Performance

Defining Key Performance Indicators (KPIs) for Categories

Key Performance Indicators (KPIs) are essential tools in category management, enabling organizations to monitor, assess, and optimize performance in a structured and measurable way. In the context of category management, KPIs are designed to align with the strategic objectives of the category and reflect the effectiveness of the execution plan. By defining KPIs for each category, organizations can ensure they are tracking the right metrics that drive value, support decision-making, and enable continuous improvement.

The first step in defining KPIs is to **align them with the overall strategic goals** of the category. This ensures that the metrics reflect the critical success factors for each category. For example, if a category strategy is focused on cost reduction, relevant KPIs might include cost savings, cost avoidance, or supplier price reductions. If the strategy is focused on quality or service improvement, KPIs might focus on supplier performance, defect rates, or delivery times. Each category may have different KPIs, depending on its unique objectives, but they should always be linked to the broader organizational goals.

It is important to ensure that KPIs are **specific, measurable, achievable, relevant, and time-bound** (SMART). Specificity ensures that the KPIs clearly define what is being measured, while measurability guarantees that the metrics can be quantified. Achievability ensures that the targets are realistic, and relevance ensures that the KPIs directly impact the category's performance. Time-bound KPIs ensure that performance can be evaluated within a defined timeframe. Examples of SMART KPIs for category management include:

- **Cost Savings:** Percentage reduction in total category spend compared to the baseline.
- **Supplier Performance:** Percentage of on-time deliveries or supplier adherence to agreed-upon quality standards.
- **Supplier Innovation:** Number of new product innovations introduced by suppliers over a year.
- **Contract Compliance:** Percentage of contract terms adhered to by suppliers.
- **Risk Mitigation:** Number of identified risks that have been mitigated or managed effectively within the category.

In addition to being SMART, KPIs should be **aligned with the entire supply chain**. Category managers should work with cross-functional teams to ensure that KPIs reflect the priorities of stakeholders such as procurement, finance, operations, and other relevant departments. This alignment fosters collaboration and ensures that everyone involved in category management is working towards the same goals.

Another important consideration is to define both **leading** and **lagging** indicators. Leading indicators are metrics that can predict future performance and allow category managers to take proactive measures to improve results. For example, tracking supplier lead times may help anticipate potential delays before they become issues. Lagging indicators, on the other hand, reflect past performance and are used to assess whether objectives were met. Examples of lagging indicators include total spend reductions or customer satisfaction scores.

Tools for Monitoring and Reporting Category Performance

Once KPIs are defined, it is essential to have effective tools and systems in place to **monitor** and **report** category performance. This is critical not only for tracking progress but also for providing real-time visibility into category management efforts, enabling better decision-making, and ensuring accountability.

One of the most widely used tools for performance monitoring is the **performance dashboard**. Dashboards provide a visual representation of KPIs and other performance metrics, allowing category managers to track performance at a glance. These dashboards often consolidate data from multiple sources into a single interface, making it easier to monitor key metrics such as cost savings, supplier performance, and contract compliance. Dashboards can be customized to suit the specific needs of the category or organization, and they can be updated in real-time to reflect the most current data. This tool helps managers quickly identify trends, spot issues, and take corrective actions if needed.

Supplier scorecards are another powerful tool for monitoring and reporting category performance. These scorecards track and evaluate supplier performance across a range of metrics, including quality, delivery, innovation, and cost. Supplier scorecards provide both quantitative data and qualitative feedback, enabling category managers to assess how well suppliers are meeting expectations. By regularly reviewing supplier scorecards, category managers can identify high-performing suppliers, recognize areas for improvement, and make data-driven decisions about supplier relationships and sourcing strategies.

For more comprehensive analysis, **spend analytics tools** are invaluable. These tools help organizations aggregate and analyze spend data across various categories and suppliers. By providing insights into purchasing patterns, price trends, and cost structures, spend analytics tools enable category managers to make more informed decisions about sourcing and procurement strategies. These tools also allow for **benchmarking** category performance against industry standards, helping organizations identify areas where they may be underperforming or could achieve greater efficiencies.

Contract management systems are essential for tracking contract compliance and performance. These systems help ensure that suppliers are meeting the terms outlined in their contracts, including pricing, delivery schedules, and quality standards. By automatically flagging non-compliance or deviations from contract terms, contract management systems provide category managers with valuable data that can be used to drive performance improvements and manage supplier relationships more effectively.

Finally, **data visualization tools** can help present category performance in a clear and accessible format. These tools allow category managers to create charts, graphs, and reports that make complex data easier to understand. Visualization helps to communicate performance to both senior management and operational teams, ensuring that key stakeholders have the insights they need to make informed decisions.

Continuous Improvement through Feedback Loops

Continuous improvement is a cornerstone of effective category management. The ultimate goal of measuring and managing performance is not only to track progress but also to create a feedback loop that fosters ongoing refinement of category strategies and execution. By continuously gathering data, evaluating performance, and making adjustments, category managers can optimize category management processes over time, driving increased value for the organization.

The first step in building a feedback loop is to establish regular performance reviews. These reviews should be scheduled at intervals throughout the year to assess the progress of category plans, evaluate performance against KPIs, and identify areas where improvement is needed. These reviews should be a collaborative process, involving key stakeholders from procurement, finance, operations, and other relevant departments. By regularly reviewing performance, category managers can identify trends, challenges, and opportunities for improvement.

During performance reviews, **root cause analysis** plays a vital role. If performance is falling short of expectations, it is essential to conduct a thorough investigation to determine the underlying causes. This analysis can reveal whether issues are due to supplier performance, internal processes, or market conditions. Once the root causes are identified, category managers can develop corrective action plans that address the underlying issues rather than just the symptoms.

Feedback should also be gathered from suppliers. **Supplier performance evaluations** are an essential part of the feedback loop, as suppliers provide valuable insights into the effectiveness of the category strategy and execution. Regular feedback from suppliers can help category managers understand what is working well and where improvements can be made, particularly in areas such as delivery schedules, quality control, or innovation.

Furthermore, **employee feedback** is another critical source of continuous improvement. Category managers should actively solicit feedback from internal teams involved in category management processes, including procurement professionals, legal, finance, and operations staff. These employees are often on the front lines of category execution and can provide valuable insights into what is working well and where improvements could be made.

Finally, **process refinement** is an ongoing part of the feedback loop. As data is collected, analyzed, and reviewed, category managers should continually assess and refine category management processes to enhance efficiency and effectiveness. This could involve adjusting sourcing strategies, renegotiating contracts, or adopting new technologies that streamline procurement operations. The goal is to create a cycle of continuous improvement that ensures category management processes are constantly evolving to meet changing market conditions, organizational goals, and supplier capabilities.

In conclusion, measuring and managing performance is an ongoing process that requires a strategic approach to KPIs, effective monitoring and reporting tools, and a commitment to continuous improvement. By defining clear and measurable KPIs, utilizing the right tools for performance tracking, and fostering a feedback loop for improvement, category managers can ensure that category strategies are successfully executed and that performance continues to improve over time, driving value for the organization.

Chapter 12: Risk Management in Categories

Identifying and Managing Procurement Risks

In category management, risk management is a critical component of ensuring the long-term success and sustainability of procurement strategies. Procurement risks can arise from a variety of sources, ranging from supply chain disruptions to geopolitical changes, and can have significant consequences on the overall category performance. The ability to identify, assess, and mitigate these risks is essential for category managers to safeguard their organization's objectives, enhance supplier relationships, and maintain competitive advantage.

The first step in risk management is to **identify potential risks** that could affect category performance. Risks in procurement can be classified into several categories, such as:

> **Supply Chain Risks**: These include disruptions in the flow of goods or services due to supplier failures, logistics issues, or natural disasters. Supply chain risks can result in delays, shortages, or quality issues that impact customer satisfaction and operational efficiency.
>
> **Market Risks**: Fluctuations in commodity prices, exchange rates, and market demand can lead to unpredictable costs and pricing instability. These risks can affect both direct and indirect procurement categories, requiring careful market analysis and forecasting to anticipate changes.
>
> **Financial Risks**: These risks involve the financial stability of suppliers or partners, which could lead to bankruptcy, liquidity crises, or delayed payments.

Financial risks often require thorough supplier assessments and regular monitoring of financial health.

Regulatory and Compliance Risks: Legal and regulatory changes, such as new labor laws, tariffs, trade regulations, or environmental standards, can affect procurement strategies and increase the cost of compliance.

Reputational Risks: The actions or failures of suppliers can affect the organization's reputation. For instance, if a supplier is involved in unethical practices or fails to meet quality standards, it could damage the organization's brand and consumer trust.

Strategic Risks: These risks are associated with the alignment of procurement strategies with broader organizational goals. Poorly executed strategies, misaligned objectives, or failure to innovate in sourcing can lead to missed opportunities or inefficiencies.

Once risks are identified, the next step is **assessing their potential impact** and likelihood. Category managers can use tools such as **risk matrices** to categorize risks based on their probability and potential impact. High-probability, high-impact risks should be prioritized, while low-probability, low-impact risks may require less attention. For example, the risk of a natural disaster impacting a supplier's operations in a remote region might be categorized as low-probability but high-impact, requiring contingency planning but not constant monitoring.

The process of managing procurement risks also involves implementing **risk mitigation strategies**. These strategies are designed to reduce the likelihood of risks occurring or minimize their impact if they do materialize. Common risk mitigation approaches include:

Diversification: Relying on multiple suppliers or sourcing from various geographic locations can reduce the risk of dependency on a single source. Diversification helps in preventing supply chain disruptions caused by a single supplier's failure or regional issues.

Supplier Risk Assessments: Regularly evaluating the financial stability, performance history, and operational capabilities of suppliers can help identify potential risks early. This allows category managers to address issues before they escalate, for example, by negotiating more flexible contract terms or finding alternative suppliers.

Contractual Safeguards: Contracts should include clauses that address potential risks, such as penalties for non-performance, clauses for price adjustments due to market changes, and force majeure clauses that cover unforeseen events like natural disasters. These clauses provide a framework for managing risks and help ensure that both parties are protected.

Inventory Management: Building buffer stocks or safety inventories for critical components or high-risk categories can help mitigate supply chain disruptions. This strategy provides a cushion against delays or shortages, ensuring business continuity.

Technology Integration: Leveraging advanced analytics, AI, and supply chain visibility tools can help anticipate risks and respond proactively. Predictive analytics can identify potential supply chain bottlenecks, quality issues, or market fluctuations, enabling category managers to act before problems arise.

Building Resilience in Category Strategies

Building resilience into category strategies is a proactive approach to risk management. A resilient category strategy is one that not only addresses risks as they arise but also anticipates challenges and is flexible enough to adapt to changing circumstances. The goal is to ensure that the category can withstand shocks and recover quickly from disruptions, thereby minimizing long-term negative impacts on the organization.

One key aspect of building resilience is **developing flexible sourcing strategies**. Rather than relying on a single supplier or a narrow set of suppliers, resilient category strategies often incorporate multiple suppliers, regions, and sourcing models. This reduces the risk of total disruption in case one supplier or region faces challenges. For example, using a mix of local and global suppliers, or implementing dual-sourcing strategies, allows companies to mitigate the risks associated with geopolitical issues, transportation disruptions, or tariffs.

Scenario planning is another important tool for building resilience. This process involves analyzing potential disruptions and developing response plans for various scenarios. For example, category managers might assess the potential impact of a natural disaster, a major supplier failure, or a sudden rise in commodity prices. By planning for these possible events, companies can be better prepared to react quickly and minimize disruptions. Scenario planning helps ensure that category managers have a clear strategy in place and are not caught off guard when risks materialize.

Another strategy for enhancing resilience is the use of **advanced technology**. Digital tools such as **Enterprise Resource Planning (ERP) systems**, **Supply Chain Management (SCM) software**, and **Supplier Relationship Management (SRM) systems** allow organizations to gain real-time visibility into supply chains and track performance across various categories. This data-driven approach helps identify potential risks earlier and enables category managers to make informed decisions that maintain business continuity. Moreover, leveraging predictive analytics can provide insights into emerging risks, allowing managers to make proactive adjustments to strategies.

Building resilience also requires a **collaborative approach with suppliers**. Strengthening relationships with key suppliers is essential for ensuring that they are also prepared for disruptions. Joint risk management strategies, regular communication, and shared contingency planning can help organizations and their suppliers develop a unified response to potential risks. For instance, a supplier might be more willing to prioritize an organization's order if they have a long-term partnership and a mutual understanding of the risks involved. Collaborative risk management also encourages innovation and problem-solving, helping both parties find creative solutions to challenges.

Lastly, creating a **culture of agility** within the category management team is vital for resilience. Agility refers to the ability of category managers to quickly adapt to changing circumstances and reassess priorities in real-time. An agile category management team can pivot quickly when risks arise, recalibrating strategies and sourcing decisions as needed. Training, cross-functional collaboration, and a mindset of continuous improvement can help foster agility across category management teams, allowing them to respond to risks more effectively.

Case Studies in Effective Risk Mitigation

To further illustrate how risk management and resilience can be applied in category management, it is helpful to explore real-world examples and case studies of organizations that have successfully mitigated procurement risks.

One such example is **Toyota's response to supply chain disruptions**. After the 2011 earthquake and tsunami in Japan, Toyota faced significant disruptions to its supply chain, particularly with suppliers of key components. In response, Toyota implemented a strategy of **supply chain diversification** by sourcing components from multiple suppliers in different regions. Toyota also strengthened its relationships with key suppliers, investing in joint risk management efforts and conducting regular scenario planning exercises. This proactive approach allowed Toyota to recover more quickly from future disruptions and to avoid severe supply chain issues in subsequent crises.

Another example is **Apple's approach to managing market risks**. Apple is known for its extensive global supply chain, which involves sourcing materials and components from multiple suppliers worldwide. In addition to diversification, Apple uses advanced technology to mitigate market risks, particularly fluctuations in commodity prices. By leveraging **predictive analytics** and sophisticated supply chain visibility tools, Apple can anticipate market shifts and adjust its procurement strategies accordingly, ensuring that it can manage costs and maintain supplier relationships even in volatile markets.

A third case study is **Unilever's supplier sustainability program**, which focuses on managing reputational and compliance risks. Unilever has worked closely with its suppliers to improve social and environmental sustainability practices, mitigating risks associated with unethical practices, labor violations, and environmental harm. Through its **Supplier Sustainability Program**, Unilever conducts regular supplier audits, provides training, and collaborates with suppliers to improve their performance. This proactive risk management strategy has helped Unilever protect its brand reputation and ensure compliance with increasingly stringent global regulations.

In each of these cases, the organizations' ability to anticipate, assess, and mitigate risks played a key role in maintaining the continuity of their category strategies. By employing a combination of diversification, advanced technology, supplier collaboration, and scenario planning, these companies were able to build resilience into their procurement strategies and navigate challenges with agility and foresight.

In conclusion, risk management in category management is not just about reacting to potential disruptions but about proactively identifying, assessing, and mitigating risks before they impact operations. By building resilience into category strategies, leveraging technology, and fostering strong relationships with suppliers, organizations can ensure that their procurement operations remain robust and adaptable, even in the face of uncertainty.

Chapter 13: Role of Digital Transformation

Procurement 4.0 and Its Impact on Category Management

In recent years, **Procurement 4.0** has emerged as a transformative concept in the procurement industry, marking a significant shift towards a more digital, data-driven, and automated approach. This new wave of procurement practices is driven by the rise of advanced technologies, such as artificial intelligence (AI), big data, cloud computing, and the Internet of Things (IoT). Procurement 4.0 represents the next stage in the evolution of category management, integrating the benefits of these digital tools to improve efficiency, enhance decision-making, and drive value across the supply chain.

One of the most significant impacts of **Procurement 4.0** on category management is the ability to move from reactive to proactive decision-making. Traditional procurement models often relied on historical data and manual processes to inform decisions, which limited their ability to respond quickly to changes in the market. In contrast, Procurement 4.0 leverages real-time data and advanced analytics to provide category managers with a deeper understanding of market conditions, supplier performance, and demand patterns. This shift enables category managers to make more informed, data-driven decisions and anticipate changes before they occur, ultimately leading to greater cost savings, improved supplier relationships, and enhanced operational efficiency.

Furthermore, the digital transformation of procurement brings increased **automation** and **intelligence** into category management processes. Tasks such as supplier selection, contract management, and order fulfillment can now be automated using AI-powered tools and algorithms, reducing the administrative burden on procurement teams and freeing up time for more strategic activities. Automation also enhances accuracy and consistency in procurement processes, reducing the risk of errors and inefficiencies. As a result, category managers can focus on higher-value tasks, such as developing long-term strategies, identifying innovation opportunities, and managing supplier relationships.

Another critical aspect of Procurement 4.0 is the **collaborative nature** of digital tools, which allow for more seamless interaction between procurement teams, suppliers, and internal stakeholders. Through cloud-based platforms and digital collaboration tools, category managers can work more closely with suppliers to share information, co-create solutions, and resolve issues in real time. This level of collaboration fosters stronger partnerships and helps to align procurement strategies with organizational goals, ultimately driving better outcomes for the business.

Leveraging Big Data, AI, and Machine Learning

The integration of **big data**, **AI**, and **machine learning** is at the heart of digital transformation in category management. These technologies allow category managers to gain deeper insights into their categories, predict trends, and optimize decision-making processes.

Big Data plays a central role in helping category managers understand market trends, supplier performance, and customer preferences. By analyzing vast amounts of structured and unstructured data, category managers can identify patterns that would be difficult or impossible to detect using traditional methods. This could include insights into spending patterns, supplier capabilities, product demand fluctuations, and even broader macroeconomic trends. For example, analyzing transactional data across various categories can reveal hidden inefficiencies in spending or opportunities for consolidation, enabling category managers to optimize sourcing decisions and reduce costs.

AI and **machine learning (ML)** are transforming the way procurement professionals make decisions. Machine learning algorithms can analyze historical data to identify trends and patterns, allowing category managers to predict future outcomes with a higher degree of accuracy. For instance, machine learning can be used to forecast demand for particular products or services, enabling category managers to align inventory levels and procurement strategies more effectively. Additionally, AI can assist in supplier evaluation by analyzing supplier performance data, financial health, and market conditions to identify the best potential partners. This automated evaluation process not only reduces the time spent on supplier selection but also enhances the accuracy and consistency of decisions.

One of the most powerful uses of AI and machine learning in category management is in **predictive analytics**. By leveraging algorithms that analyze historical and real-time data, category managers can forecast potential risks and opportunities within their categories. For instance, AI can predict price volatility, potential supplier disruptions, or changes in consumer demand, allowing category managers to adjust their strategies proactively. Predictive models can also be used to optimize sourcing decisions, such as identifying the best suppliers for a particular category based on historical performance data and market conditions.

Furthermore, AI-powered **chatbots** and **virtual assistants** are helping to automate routine tasks such as responding to supplier inquiries, generating purchase orders, and tracking delivery statuses. These tools improve efficiency, reduce administrative workload, and enhance communication between category managers, suppliers, and internal stakeholders.

Tools for Digital Category Management

To fully leverage the benefits of digital transformation, category managers need access to a suite of digital tools that enable them to manage their categories more effectively. These tools help streamline processes, enhance decision-making, and improve collaboration across the procurement function.

One of the most essential tools in digital category management is **Procurement Software**. Modern procurement platforms offer a wide range of functionalities, including supplier management, contract management, sourcing, procurement analytics, and procurement automation. These platforms centralize procurement activities, allowing category managers to access real-time data and collaborate with internal and external stakeholders more effectively. Additionally, procurement software enables more efficient supplier relationship management by providing tools for evaluating supplier performance, tracking supplier risks, and ensuring compliance with contract terms.

Supplier Relationship Management (SRM) Systems are another crucial tool in digital category management. SRM systems provide category managers with a comprehensive view of supplier performance, including quality metrics, delivery performance, and financial stability. By maintaining a centralized supplier database, category managers can track key supplier performance indicators, monitor contract compliance, and identify opportunities for supplier collaboration. SRM systems also enable better communication and collaboration with suppliers, facilitating joint innovation and problem-solving.

In addition to SRM systems, category managers can use **Spend Analytics Tools** to analyze procurement spending data. These tools use big data analytics to track spending patterns, identify opportunities for cost savings, and optimize supplier selection. Spend analytics tools can help category managers identify high-spend areas, track supplier performance over time, and highlight opportunities for category consolidation or renegotiation of contracts. By having visibility into spending trends and supplier behavior, category managers can make more strategic decisions that align with the organization's goals.

Contract Management Software is another critical tool for digital category management. This software allows category managers to automate the contract creation, review, and approval processes, reducing administrative time and ensuring compliance with organizational standards. Contract management tools also provide greater visibility into contract performance, helping category managers track milestones, delivery terms, and renewals. Additionally, these tools allow for greater risk management by storing contract terms, legal clauses, and compliance requirements in a centralized system that is easily accessible.

Cloud-Based Platforms are transforming the way category managers collaborate with internal teams and external suppliers. By using cloud-based platforms, category managers can access real-time data, share documents, and communicate with stakeholders from anywhere in the world. This enhanced collaboration improves efficiency, reduces delays, and ensures that all parties are aligned on procurement goals. Cloud-based platforms also provide scalability, enabling category managers to manage categories of any size, whether global or local, with ease.

Finally, **Artificial Intelligence (AI)-Powered Decision Support Tools** are becoming an essential part of digital category management. These tools use AI algorithms to analyze vast amounts of data and provide recommendations on sourcing decisions, supplier selection, pricing strategies, and contract negotiations. AI-powered decision support tools enable category managers to make faster, more informed decisions, reducing the time required for manual data analysis and enhancing overall procurement performance.

The Future of Digital Category Management

As digital transformation continues to reshape category management, the future of procurement looks increasingly automated, data-driven, and collaborative. The adoption of **Robotic Process Automation (RPA)**, **blockchain technology**, and **IoT** is expected to further enhance procurement processes, driving greater transparency, efficiency, and traceability across the supply chain. For instance, blockchain could be used to improve transparency in supplier relationships, allowing category managers to verify product authenticity and track goods as they move through the supply chain.

Additionally, the use of **advanced analytics** and **predictive modeling** will continue to improve decision-making, allowing category managers to anticipate market changes, mitigate risks, and optimize procurement strategies. As AI and machine learning evolve, these technologies will become even more powerful, enabling category managers to automate routine tasks, predict demand fluctuations, and make real-time adjustments to sourcing strategies.

In conclusion, digital transformation is revolutionizing category management, providing category managers with the tools and technologies they need to improve decision-making, enhance efficiency, and drive value for their organizations. By embracing technologies such as AI, big data, and machine learning, procurement professionals can move beyond traditional practices and unlock new opportunities for growth and innovation in the category management function. As procurement becomes more integrated into the broader digital ecosystem, category managers will be better equipped to navigate the complexities of modern supply chains and deliver lasting value to their organizations.

Chapter 14: Automating Category Management

Benefits of Automation in Procurement Processes

The procurement industry, like many other sectors, has undergone significant transformations in recent years. One of the key drivers of this transformation is automation, which is reshaping the way category management is conducted. The integration of automation into procurement processes offers a multitude of benefits, ranging from enhanced efficiency to cost savings, greater transparency, and improved decision-making.

One of the most significant benefits of automation in category management is **improved operational efficiency**. Traditionally, procurement professionals spent a substantial amount of time on repetitive, manual tasks, such as processing purchase orders, tracking supplier performance, and managing contracts. Automation tools are designed to handle these tasks quickly and accurately, reducing the time required for administrative work. For example, an automated procurement system can instantly generate purchase orders based on predefined criteria, ensuring that requisitions are processed without the need for manual intervention. As a result, category managers can focus on more strategic activities, such as supplier relationship management, category strategy development, and cost optimization.

Automation also provides **greater accuracy and consistency** in procurement activities. Human error, such as data entry mistakes or overlooking contract terms, can lead to costly errors and inefficiencies. Automated systems, on the other hand, follow predefined rules and workflows, reducing the likelihood of such mistakes. For instance, automated spend analysis tools can quickly analyze large volumes of transactional data to identify spending patterns, detect anomalies, and flag potential areas for cost savings. By automating data entry and analysis, category managers can trust that the information they are working with is accurate, which enhances decision-making and ensures compliance with organizational policies.

Another key advantage of automation is **cost savings**. By streamlining procurement processes, organizations can reduce overhead costs associated with manual labor, paper-based workflows, and inefficient supplier management. For example, automated procurement systems eliminate the need for paper-based purchase orders, reducing administrative costs related to printing, filing, and storing physical documents. Additionally, automated tools enable category managers to more effectively track supplier performance and manage contracts, ensuring that suppliers meet agreed-upon terms and conditions, which can help prevent cost overruns and delays. Over time, these cost savings accumulate, contributing to improved bottom-line results.

Beyond cost reduction, automation also supports **better data visibility**. In manual procurement systems, data is often siloed in different departments or spreadsheets, making it difficult for category managers to gain a comprehensive view of procurement activities. Automation consolidates data into centralized systems, offering category managers real-time insights into spending, supplier performance, and procurement trends. This transparency helps category managers identify areas of inefficiency, track key performance indicators (KPIs), and make data-driven decisions that align with the organization's overall objectives. In addition, automated systems often include powerful reporting tools that generate real-time dashboards and analytical reports, allowing category managers to monitor the performance of their categories continuously.

Lastly, automation fosters **enhanced supplier relationships**. Automated systems allow for better communication and collaboration between procurement teams and suppliers. For instance, e-procurement systems can facilitate real-time order tracking, ensuring that suppliers are notified of any changes to purchase orders immediately. Automated systems also improve the accuracy and timeliness of payments, which can help strengthen supplier relationships and foster long-term partnerships. Furthermore, category managers can use automated tools to assess supplier performance continuously, enabling them to identify and address any issues promptly.

Examples: e-Procurement, Spend Analytics, and Category Dashboards

The concept of automation in category management encompasses a variety of tools and technologies designed to streamline different aspects of the procurement process. Some of the most common examples of automation tools include **e-procurement systems**, **spend analytics tools**, and **category dashboards**.

e-Procurement Systems are perhaps the most widely used automation tools in modern procurement. These systems automate the entire procurement lifecycle, from requisition to payment. With e-procurement, purchasing departments can automate tasks such as generating purchase orders, receiving electronic invoices, and managing approvals. Additionally, e-procurement systems often integrate with suppliers' systems, allowing for seamless order fulfillment and reducing the potential for errors in the procurement process. By digitizing the entire procurement process, e-procurement systems help reduce the reliance on paper-based workflows and streamline the entire purchasing function, improving both efficiency and compliance.

Spend Analytics is another key area where automation is having a significant impact. Spend analytics tools automatically collect and analyze procurement data from various sources, such as invoices, purchase orders, and supplier contracts. These tools provide category managers with a detailed, real-time view of spending patterns, supplier performance, and opportunities for cost savings. For example, automated spend analytics tools can identify trends in supplier pricing, flag high-spend categories, and highlight areas where consolidation or renegotiation may be beneficial. By automating the process of spend analysis, category managers can gain actionable insights quickly, enabling them to make more informed decisions that contribute to greater cost efficiency and strategic sourcing.

Category Dashboards are a powerful tool for monitoring and reporting category performance. These dashboards provide real-time, visual representations of key performance indicators (KPIs) related to specific categories. For example, category dashboards can display metrics such as total spend, supplier performance, contract compliance, and cost savings. By automating the process of tracking and reporting these metrics, category managers can quickly assess the health of their categories and take corrective action when necessary. Category dashboards not only improve visibility into procurement performance but also support data-driven decision-making by providing category managers with real-time access to relevant information.

Another example of automation in category management is the use of **automated contract management systems**. These systems streamline the contract lifecycle, from creation and negotiation to execution and compliance monitoring. Automated contract management tools ensure that contracts are executed according to agreed-upon terms, reducing the risk of errors and improving compliance. These systems can also include automated reminders for contract renewals, enabling category managers to stay on top of critical contract deadlines and renegotiation opportunities.

Overcoming Challenges in Automation

Despite the many benefits of automation in category management, organizations often face challenges in implementing and adopting automated systems. One of the most common challenges is **resistance to change**. Many procurement professionals are accustomed to traditional, manual processes and may be hesitant to adopt new technologies. To overcome this resistance, it is essential for organizations to invest in **change management** initiatives, such as training and communication programs, to ensure that employees are comfortable with the new systems and understand the benefits of automation.

Another challenge is the **initial investment** required to implement automation tools. While automation can lead to significant long-term cost savings, the upfront costs associated with acquiring and integrating new technologies can be a barrier for some organizations. To address this challenge, organizations can look for cost-effective solutions, such as cloud-based procurement tools, which offer flexibility and scalability without the need for large upfront investments. Additionally, organizations should focus on the long-term return on investment (ROI) when evaluating automation tools, as the benefits often outweigh the initial costs over time.

Data **integration** is another key challenge when implementing automation in category management. Many organizations rely on disparate systems for different aspects of procurement, such as supplier management, purchasing, and contract management. Integrating these systems to work seamlessly together can be a complex and time-consuming process. To address this, organizations should prioritize systems that offer integration capabilities and work with experienced IT professionals to ensure that their automated tools can communicate effectively across different platforms.

Finally, **data security** is a critical concern when automating procurement processes. Since procurement data often includes sensitive information such as supplier contracts, pricing details, and financial data, it is essential to implement robust security measures to protect this information. Organizations must ensure that their automation tools adhere to industry-standard security protocols and comply with data privacy regulations.

In conclusion, automation is transforming category management by improving efficiency, accuracy, and transparency in procurement processes. By embracing automation tools such as e-procurement systems, spend analytics, and category dashboards, category managers can enhance their decision-making, drive cost savings, and foster stronger supplier relationships. However, organizations must also be mindful of the challenges associated with automation, including resistance to change, initial investment costs, data integration, and security concerns. By carefully planning and implementing automation strategies, organizations can unlock the full potential of category management and stay ahead in an increasingly competitive and fast-paced business environment.

Chapter 15: Sustainable and Ethical Sourcing

Incorporating Sustainability into Category Strategies

Sustainability has become an essential consideration for organizations across industries. As awareness of environmental and social challenges grows, companies are increasingly expected to adopt sustainable practices in their procurement and supply chain activities. Category managers play a critical role in integrating sustainability into their category strategies, ensuring that sourcing decisions contribute to both long-term value creation and responsible business practices.

Incorporating sustainability into category strategies begins with understanding the **environmental and social impact** of the products or services being procured. A category manager needs to assess the entire lifecycle of a product, from raw material extraction to production, transportation, and disposal, to identify opportunities for reducing environmental footprints. This involves considering factors such as **carbon emissions**, **resource usage**, and **waste generation** in the decision-making process.

The first step is to **align sustainability goals with business objectives**. Companies that are committed to sustainability typically have formal sustainability goals, which may include reducing greenhouse gas emissions, increasing the use of renewable energy, or achieving zero waste. It is the responsibility of category managers to integrate these sustainability targets into their category strategies. For instance, a category manager may prioritize sourcing from suppliers who utilize renewable energy or implement waste-reduction initiatives in their production processes. They may also set goals for using **sustainable materials** or reduce reliance on single-use plastics, which are common sustainability concerns.

Collaboration with stakeholders—both internally and externally—plays a crucial role in implementing sustainable sourcing strategies. Category managers must work closely with other departments such as **supply chain**, **product development**, and **corporate social responsibility (CSR)** teams to ensure that sustainability is a top priority. Engaging suppliers is also essential. Suppliers who share the company's sustainability values are more likely to collaborate on long-term projects aimed at improving the environmental and social performance of the supply chain.

One of the key components of sustainable sourcing is adopting a **circular economy** model, which emphasizes the reuse and recycling of materials to minimize waste and reduce the need for virgin resources. For example, category managers may look for suppliers who design products for durability, reuse, or recycling. They may also work with suppliers to establish reverse logistics systems, allowing products to be returned for refurbishment, repair, or recycling.

Furthermore, category managers can utilize **sustainability certifications** and **standards** to guide their sourcing decisions. Various organizations and initiatives, such as the **Fair Trade** certification, **Forest Stewardship Council (FSC)**, and **Global Reporting Initiative (GRI)**, offer recognized standards for sustainable practices. Leveraging these certifications provides a clear framework for sourcing materials and services that meet high sustainability criteria.

Ethical Procurement Practices: Avoiding Modern Slavery and Corruption

Ethical sourcing is a critical component of a responsible procurement strategy. Procurement professionals, especially category managers, must be vigilant in ensuring that the supply chain is free from unethical practices such as **modern slavery**, **child labor**, and **corruption**. These issues not only undermine human rights but can also harm the reputation and legal standing of organizations.

To address these concerns, category managers should establish **rigorous supplier selection and evaluation criteria**. This includes assessing the ethical practices of potential suppliers, particularly in regions where the risk of modern slavery and unethical labor practices is higher. One of the first steps is to **conduct due diligence** on suppliers to ensure that they adhere to ethical labor practices. This can be achieved by requiring suppliers to sign a **Supplier Code of Conduct** that explicitly prohibits forced labor, child labor, and discrimination. Category managers should also assess suppliers' commitment to fair wages, safe working conditions, and respect for workers' rights.

Regular audits and assessments are essential to ensure that suppliers comply with these standards. These audits can be conducted by third-party organizations specializing in ethical sourcing or through internal teams trained to identify risks in the supply chain. For example, auditors can visit supplier facilities to verify working conditions and ensure that employees are not subjected to unfair treatment. Category managers should work with suppliers to implement corrective actions when ethical violations are discovered and consider **alternative sourcing options** if necessary.

Another key aspect of ethical procurement is **avoiding corruption**. This includes ensuring that all procurement activities are free from bribery, fraud, and unethical financial dealings. Category managers can mitigate corruption risks by adhering to **anti-corruption policies** and **anti-bribery regulations** such as the **Foreign Corrupt Practices Act (FCPA)** and the **UK Bribery Act**. These regulations outline stringent guidelines for transparent procurement activities and hold organizations accountable for preventing corrupt practices. Ensuring transparency in supplier relationships, tendering processes, and contract management can help reduce the risk of corruption.

Category managers can also implement **whistleblowing mechanisms**, which encourage employees and suppliers to report unethical behavior without fear of retaliation. Providing these channels for reporting concerns can help identify potential ethical violations early and take corrective action promptly. Additionally, providing training to procurement professionals, suppliers, and other stakeholders about ethical sourcing standards and legal requirements helps ensure a shared commitment to ethical procurement practices.

Measuring and Reporting on Sustainability Goals

Measuring and reporting on sustainability goals is critical for ensuring accountability and transparency in category management. Companies need to demonstrate the progress they are making toward their sustainability objectives to stakeholders, including investors, customers, and regulatory bodies. This involves establishing a clear framework for measuring sustainability outcomes and using accurate, data-driven reporting tools.

The first step in measuring sustainability goals is to define **key performance indicators (KPIs)** that align with the organization's sustainability targets. These KPIs should be specific, measurable, achievable, relevant, and time-bound (SMART). For example, if the company's goal is to reduce carbon emissions, the KPIs could include metrics such as **carbon footprint reduction** per unit of production, **percentage of renewable energy used**, or **emissions avoided** through sustainable sourcing practices.

Category managers should work closely with data analytics teams to ensure that relevant data is collected, tracked, and analyzed regularly. This might involve leveraging **sustainability software tools** that aggregate data from various sources across the supply chain. These tools can help track the environmental and social performance of suppliers, monitor energy usage, and measure waste reduction, among other factors. By automating the data collection process, category managers can more easily monitor performance in real-time and make adjustments as needed.

Once the data has been collected, it must be reported in a transparent and consistent manner. Reporting tools, such as **sustainability dashboards**, provide visual representations of performance against sustainability goals, enabling category managers and senior leaders to assess progress quickly. These dashboards can also help in benchmarking performance against industry standards or competitor performance.

In addition to internal reporting, category managers must also focus on **external reporting** to demonstrate their commitment to sustainability and ethical sourcing. This could involve publishing **annual sustainability reports**, participating in **sustainability indices** (such as the **Dow Jones Sustainability Index**), and disclosing information about sourcing practices to customers and investors. Many organizations now voluntarily submit sustainability data to frameworks like the **Global Reporting Initiative (GRI)** or **Sustainable Development Goals (SDGs)**, both of which offer recognized standards for sustainability reporting.

Third-party certifications and **auditing** also play an essential role in verifying sustainability claims. Category managers can work with third-party organizations to certify the environmental and ethical practices of suppliers, ensuring that the company's sustainability reports reflect actual performance. For example, certifications like **ISO 14001** for environmental management or **Fair Trade certification** for ethical labor practices can lend credibility to sustainability claims and demonstrate a commitment to responsible sourcing.

Finally, regular reviews of sustainability strategies and KPIs are necessary to ensure that goals are being met and to identify areas for improvement. This process should include a comprehensive evaluation of the supply chain's environmental and social performance, as well as an analysis of supplier relationships and sourcing strategies. By continuously monitoring and improving sustainability practices, category managers can drive long-term value creation while contributing to global sustainability efforts.

In conclusion, sustainable and ethical sourcing is no longer just a "nice-to-have" but an essential component of modern category management. By incorporating sustainability into category strategies, adopting ethical procurement practices, and establishing robust systems for measuring and reporting sustainability goals, category managers can contribute significantly to their organizations' social, environmental, and economic performance. Ethical sourcing not only mitigates risks and enhances brand reputation but also drives long-term value, aligning business objectives with the growing demand for sustainability in the global marketplace.

Chapter 16: Category Management in Different Industries

Category management is a universal concept that applies across all industries, though its specific applications can vary based on the unique characteristics and requirements of each sector. In this chapter, we will explore how category management is implemented in different industries, including manufacturing and raw materials, retail and consumer goods, and pharmaceuticals and healthcare. We will examine the challenges faced in each sector, the strategies employed, and the benefits realized by adopting a category management approach.

Manufacturing and Raw Materials

In the manufacturing industry, category management plays a crucial role in optimizing the procurement of raw materials, components, and services required for production. The manufacturing sector is often characterized by complex supply chains, long lead times, and a reliance on various suppliers for raw materials. Category managers in this industry are responsible for identifying, evaluating, and selecting suppliers that offer the best value while ensuring that production processes are not disrupted by material shortages, delays, or quality issues.

One of the first challenges faced in manufacturing procurement is the **volatile nature of raw material prices**. The prices of raw materials such as metals, plastics, and chemicals can fluctuate significantly due to supply chain disruptions, geopolitical factors, and changes in demand. Category managers in this sector need to implement **strategic sourcing** techniques that allow them to negotiate favorable long-term contracts with suppliers, secure bulk purchasing agreements, or implement hedging strategies to protect against price volatility. By doing so, manufacturers can stabilize their material costs and ensure consistency in production costs.

Another key consideration in manufacturing category management is the **quality and consistency of raw materials**. High-quality materials are essential for producing finished goods that meet customer expectations and regulatory standards. Category managers must evaluate suppliers not only based on price but also on their ability to provide high-quality materials with consistent specifications. This involves conducting thorough **supplier assessments**, including audits and quality control checks, and establishing clear **quality standards** and **performance metrics** in supplier contracts.

Additionally, category managers in manufacturing must consider **supply chain risk management**. Given the complexity of global supply chains, manufacturing companies are exposed to risks related to natural disasters, geopolitical instability, and labor strikes. A well-structured category management process allows organizations to identify potential risks early and develop contingency plans. For example, manufacturers may work with multiple suppliers for the same raw material to ensure that any disruptions from one supplier do not halt production. Similarly, they may adopt **sustainable sourcing** practices to minimize dependency on single-source suppliers and reduce risks related to resource scarcity or ethical concerns.

Retail and Consumer Goods

The retail and consumer goods industry is characterized by its fast-paced nature and the need to respond quickly to changing consumer demands, trends, and preferences. In this sector, category management is essential for managing a wide array of products, ranging from apparel and electronics to food and beverages. Category managers in retail focus on developing strategies that improve product availability, pricing, and assortment, while driving profitability and customer satisfaction.

A key focus area in retail category management is **inventory optimization**. Retailers face the challenge of balancing the availability of products with minimizing excess inventory. Poor inventory management can lead to stockouts, which result in missed sales opportunities, or overstocking, which increases storage costs and the risk of markdowns. Category managers use sophisticated tools such as **demand forecasting** and **sales data analysis** to determine the optimal inventory levels for each product category. By aligning inventory with expected demand patterns, category managers ensure that the right products are available at the right time, helping to maximize sales and minimize waste.

Vendor relationships also play a crucial role in retail category management. Retailers often deal with a wide range of suppliers and brands, and category managers must develop strong relationships with these suppliers to secure favorable terms, access exclusive products, and stay ahead of market trends. Effective supplier collaboration can lead to **joint marketing initiatives**, **special promotions**, and **category-specific discounts**, which help to differentiate products and improve competitiveness. Retailers may also use category management to introduce **private label products** that can offer higher margins and greater control over quality and pricing.

Additionally, category managers in retail must continually assess **consumer behavior trends** and **market conditions** to ensure that the product assortment meets customer preferences. In today's digital age, e-commerce is an increasingly important channel, and category managers must incorporate **omni-channel strategies** into their category plans. This means ensuring that products are available not only in physical stores but also online, through marketplaces, or via third-party platforms. Retail category managers must work closely with **digital marketing** teams to ensure alignment between product offerings and marketing campaigns, ensuring that the right products are promoted to the right customer segments.

Pharmaceuticals and Healthcare

In the pharmaceuticals and healthcare industry, category management takes on an added layer of complexity due to regulatory requirements, product safety concerns, and the critical nature of the products being procured. Category managers in this sector deal with the procurement of pharmaceutical products, medical devices, and healthcare services, all of which must meet stringent safety and quality standards.

A significant challenge in pharmaceutical procurement is the need to **comply with regulatory standards**. The procurement of pharmaceutical products is governed by strict regulations from bodies such as the **Food and Drug Administration (FDA)**, the **European Medicines Agency (EMA)**, and other regulatory agencies worldwide. Category managers must ensure that all suppliers meet these regulatory requirements and that products are sourced from reputable manufacturers who adhere to **Good Manufacturing Practices (GMP)**. Additionally, they must track product recalls and ensure that suppliers are compliant with the latest health and safety standards.

Another unique aspect of category management in pharmaceuticals is the need to address **pricing and reimbursement issues**. Pharmaceutical products, especially patented drugs, can be highly expensive, and category managers must work to manage the cost of goods while also ensuring that the products are available to patients at an affordable price. This involves negotiating **pricing agreements** with suppliers and considering factors such as **bulk purchasing**, **volume discounts**, and **group purchasing organizations (GPOs)** to secure the best pricing for healthcare providers. At the same time, category managers must work with payers, such as insurance companies and government bodies, to ensure that the products are covered under reimbursement schemes, making them accessible to the broader patient population.

Supply chain reliability is another critical consideration in the pharmaceutical industry. Given the **time-sensitive nature** of healthcare delivery, category managers must ensure that critical products, such as life-saving medications and medical devices, are always available when needed. This requires careful planning and risk management to prevent **supply chain disruptions**, which could lead to shortages of essential products. For example, pharmaceutical category managers often establish **strategic supplier relationships** with backup suppliers and implement **contingency plans** to mitigate risks related to natural disasters, political instability, or transportation delays.

Furthermore, category managers in the healthcare sector must be proactive in addressing **sustainability** and **ethical sourcing**. In recent years, there has been increasing pressure on pharmaceutical companies to ensure that their sourcing practices align with sustainability goals. This includes sourcing materials and ingredients from suppliers who prioritize **ethical labor practices** and **environmental responsibility**. Category managers are also encouraged to assess the **environmental impact** of products, such as the **carbon footprint** of manufacturing processes or the **disposal of medical waste**.

Category management in different industries highlights the versatility and value of the category management approach.

Whether in manufacturing, retail, or pharmaceuticals, category managers play a key role in driving strategic procurement decisions that contribute to cost savings, risk mitigation, and overall organizational success. By applying tailored strategies that consider the unique challenges and requirements of each sector, category managers can optimize their supply chains, enhance supplier relationships, and ensure that their companies are equipped to meet both current and future market demands. Through the application of robust category management processes, organizations can maintain a competitive edge, achieve long-term profitability, and deliver value to customers and stakeholders alike.

Chapter 17: Global Category Management

Category management is a strategic approach that has proven successful in various industries across the globe. However, when scaled to a global level, it involves unique challenges that require a comprehensive understanding of multi-regional environments, local market conditions, and cross-border regulations. This chapter explores the key considerations for managing categories in a global context, emphasizing how organizations can navigate the complexities of global sourcing, adapt to diverse markets, and manage category strategies across different regions to ensure global success.

Managing Categories in Multi-Regional Environments

In today's interconnected world, many organizations operate across multiple regions, sourcing products and services from a diverse range of markets. Managing categories in such a multi-regional environment demands a **strategic, collaborative approach** that aligns both global and local objectives. The key challenge lies in balancing the **standardization** of procurement processes with the

localization required to meet the diverse needs of different markets.

One of the first steps in global category management is establishing a **global category management framework** that provides clear guidelines, processes, and performance metrics across all regions. This global framework helps to ensure consistency in procurement strategies and ensures that best practices are followed regardless of geographic location. However, while a global framework is important for creating efficiencies, it must also allow for flexibility to adapt to local market dynamics. Each region may have its own set of suppliers, economic conditions, and customer demands, which necessitate adjustments to procurement strategies.

For example, a **global procurement team** may oversee the purchasing of raw materials or products from different regions, but local category managers will need to execute the procurement strategies in alignment with regional supplier capabilities and market conditions. The global team can set overarching goals for cost savings, risk mitigation, and supplier relationship management, while the regional teams can tailor these objectives to the local business environment. Coordination and **collaboration** between global and regional teams are essential to ensure alignment with organizational goals and the efficient execution of category management processes.

In managing categories across multiple regions, it is essential to understand the **diverse market conditions** in each region. These may include varying levels of supplier maturity, pricing structures, and logistics capabilities. For instance, a category manager in North America may focus on sourcing from well-established suppliers with advanced logistics networks, while a counterpart in Asia may prioritize working with a different set of suppliers with varying levels of infrastructure. The ability to manage this diversity and adapt category strategies to these regional differences is essential for the success of a global category management strategy.

Adapting to Local Markets and Regulations

Adapting category management to local markets requires more than just understanding regional market conditions; it also involves navigating the complex landscape of **local regulations** and **cultural nuances** that affect procurement decisions. Each country or region has its own set of regulations regarding procurement practices, supplier qualifications, labor laws, environmental standards, and corporate governance. These local regulations can significantly impact how categories are managed and require that category managers stay abreast of **legal requirements** and compliance standards in each market.

In the European Union, for example, procurement regulations are governed by a set of directives that emphasize transparency, fairness, and competition in public procurement processes. In contrast, procurement practices in Asia may involve less regulatory oversight but place a stronger emphasis on **relationship building** and **negotiation** with suppliers. Category managers must be aware of these differences to ensure that their strategies are compliant with local laws and are effectively adapted to local business practices.

For example, in markets such as the United States and Europe, there is a significant emphasis on **environmental and sustainability regulations**, which impact the sourcing of raw materials, particularly in industries such as construction, agriculture, and manufacturing. In other regions, such as emerging markets in Africa or Southeast Asia, category managers may encounter regulatory challenges related to trade tariffs, customs, and local government restrictions. In such environments, it is important for category managers to stay closely aligned with legal teams, local stakeholders, and external regulatory bodies to ensure compliance and mitigate the risk of non-compliance penalties.

Beyond regulations, cultural differences also play a significant role in adapting category strategies to local markets. In some regions, business relationships may be based on **long-term partnerships**, while in others, there may be a stronger focus on transactional agreements. Understanding these cultural nuances is critical to fostering successful supplier relationships, negotiating effectively, and aligning procurement strategies with local business customs. For example, in Latin America and parts of Asia, there may be a greater emphasis on **personal relationships and trust** in business transactions, which may require category managers to engage in more face-to-face meetings, social interactions, and building rapport with suppliers.

Additionally, **local economic conditions**—such as inflation rates, currency fluctuations, and political stability—can impact the procurement process. Category managers need to be proactive in understanding these conditions, as they can affect supplier pricing, contract terms, and the overall cost of goods. For example, during times of high inflation or currency devaluation in certain countries, category managers may need to renegotiate contracts, adjust payment terms, or explore alternative suppliers in more stable markets to maintain cost-effectiveness.

Best Practices for Global Sourcing

Global sourcing is an essential element of category management, allowing organizations to access a wide range of suppliers, reduce costs, and ensure a steady supply of goods and services. However, global sourcing comes with its own set of risks and challenges, such as geopolitical instability, supply chain disruptions, and quality assurance concerns. To navigate these challenges, category managers must adopt best practices that ensure the effective management of global sourcing efforts.

One of the best practices for global sourcing is **supplier diversification**. Relying on a single supplier for a critical category can expose the organization to significant risks, such as supply chain disruptions or quality issues. By diversifying the supplier base across different regions, category managers can mitigate these risks and ensure continuity of supply. This approach also allows organizations to benefit from competitive pricing, as suppliers from different regions may offer varying price points based on local economic conditions and labor costs.

Another best practice is the use of **strategic supplier relationships**. Building strong, long-term relationships with suppliers is key to ensuring reliable, high-quality products and services. Category managers should focus on selecting suppliers that align with the company's values and sustainability goals, and they should invest in collaborative partnerships that go beyond transactional agreements. This can include joint product development, supplier innovation programs, and shared risk management initiatives. By developing a deeper level of collaboration, organizations can ensure that suppliers are invested in the success of the business and are motivated to deliver optimal value.

In addition to supplier relationships, category managers must consider the **total cost of ownership (TCO)** when evaluating suppliers in a global sourcing context. While lower upfront costs may be an attractive option, category managers should evaluate other factors such as shipping costs, customs duties, inventory carrying costs, and potential tariffs. By considering the full range of costs associated with global sourcing, category managers can make more informed decisions and avoid surprises in the procurement process.

To effectively manage global sourcing, it is also essential for category managers to leverage **advanced procurement technologies**. Technologies such as **e-procurement platforms**, **spend analytics tools**, and **supplier portals** can streamline the global sourcing process, improve visibility into supplier performance, and facilitate better communication across geographies. These tools allow category managers to gather and analyze data from multiple markets, track supplier performance in real-time, and make data-driven decisions that optimize the global procurement strategy.

Additionally, **risk management** is an important aspect of global sourcing. Political instability, natural disasters, and economic fluctuations in supplier countries can disrupt supply chains and impact procurement timelines. Category managers should implement risk management strategies such as **multi-sourcing**, **geopolitical risk assessments**, and **contingency planning** to minimize these risks. Establishing close relationships with local logistics providers, warehousing facilities, and third-party risk management experts can help category managers better anticipate and mitigate potential disruptions.

Global category management requires a nuanced approach that balances the need for standardized procurement processes with the flexibility to adapt to local market conditions and regulations. By managing categories across regions effectively, organizations can access a broader supplier base, reduce costs, and ensure a reliable supply of goods and services. Best practices for global sourcing, including supplier diversification, strategic supplier relationships, and TCO evaluation, are essential for optimizing procurement processes on a global scale. Moreover, category managers must stay proactive in managing risks associated with geopolitical factors, regulatory changes, and cultural differences. By embracing these strategies and practices, organizations can unlock the full potential of global category management, drive competitive advantage, and enhance their overall procurement performance in an increasingly interconnected world.

Chapter 18: Collaboration Across the Organization

In modern organizations, category management has evolved from a purely procurement-focused activity to a more integrated, cross-functional process that requires collaboration across various departments. The success of category management largely depends on effective communication, shared goals, and alignment between functions such as finance, legal, operations, and other business units. This chapter explores the role of cross-functional teams in driving category success, the importance of building strong partnerships with key departments, and strategies for overcoming internal resistance to change.

Role of Cross-Functional Teams in Category Success

Category management is inherently a **cross-functional activity** that involves collaboration between multiple stakeholders across the organization. The role of **cross-functional teams** is to provide expertise, insights, and resources that contribute to the strategic management and execution of category plans. Successful category management requires input from departments like finance, legal, operations, marketing, and supply chain, all of which offer distinct perspectives that are critical for optimizing procurement processes and achieving business objectives.

One of the key factors that determine the success of a category management initiative is the **alignment of objectives** between all involved teams. For example, while procurement teams are focused on sourcing and supplier management, finance teams are concerned with cost control, budget alignment, and financial forecasting. Legal departments must ensure compliance with contract terms and regulatory requirements, while operations teams are focused on the practical implementation of category strategies, such as ensuring the right products are available at the right time. Collaboration across these functions helps to ensure that category management strategies are **comprehensive** and **aligned** with the organization's overall goals.

Cross-functional teams facilitate better decision-making by bringing together diverse skill sets and knowledge. For example, a finance team can provide insights into **budget constraints**, helping category managers make more informed decisions on sourcing strategies. Operations teams can offer valuable input on the **practical implications** of category strategies, such as **inventory management**, product delivery timelines, and supplier performance. By working together, cross-functional teams can develop more effective category plans that balance cost, quality, risk, and operational feasibility.

Collaboration also ensures **holistic solutions** to procurement challenges. For instance, if a procurement team faces issues with a supplier's ability to meet delivery deadlines, operations can work with procurement to assess alternative sources of supply or adjust production schedules. Similarly, legal teams can help mitigate risks by reviewing contracts with suppliers and ensuring that terms are aligned with organizational requirements. These types of **synergies** are critical for ensuring that category management strategies deliver the desired outcomes and avoid operational disruptions.

Building Partnerships with Finance, Legal, and Operations

To drive category success, category managers must focus on building **strong partnerships** with key internal stakeholders, particularly in finance, legal, and operations. These relationships are foundational to the effective execution of category strategies and require proactive engagement, mutual respect, and a clear understanding of each department's objectives.

- **Partnership with Finance**: Finance plays a crucial role in the category management process, as it provides the necessary financial oversight to ensure that procurement decisions align with the organization's budget and financial goals. Category managers should regularly engage with finance teams to set financial targets for categories, establish cost-saving initiatives, and develop forecasting models based on procurement data. Finance can also help track performance against financial metrics, such as **total cost of ownership (TCO)** and **return on investment (ROI)**, to evaluate the effectiveness of category strategies. A close partnership with finance ensures that category managers have the resources they need to make cost-effective procurement decisions while staying within budget constraints.

One of the ways category managers can strengthen their partnership with finance is by demonstrating how category management contributes to **cost optimization** and **value creation**. For example, a category manager can show how strategic supplier negotiations or bulk purchasing agreements lead to cost reductions over time. By aligning category strategies with broader financial goals, category managers can create a shared sense of purpose and foster stronger collaboration with finance teams.

- **Partnership with Legal**: Legal teams are instrumental in ensuring that category management processes comply with local laws, regulatory requirements, and contractual obligations.

Collaborating with legal teams is essential when drafting and negotiating supplier contracts, reviewing terms and conditions, and managing risks associated with procurement activities. Legal experts can also provide valuable guidance on how to structure **risk mitigation clauses** in contracts, such as penalties for non-performance or the inclusion of **force majeure** provisions to protect against unforeseen disruptions in the supply chain.

In addition to contract management, legal teams can help mitigate risks related to **ethics**, **compliance**, and **anti-corruption laws**. They can assist in ensuring that suppliers adhere to standards related to human rights, labor laws, environmental practices, and anti-bribery policies. As category managers increasingly focus on **sustainability** and **ethical sourcing**, a partnership with legal is critical to ensuring that procurement strategies align with both the organization's values and external regulations.

- **Partnership with Operations**: Operations teams are directly involved in the execution of category management strategies and are responsible for ensuring that procurement decisions translate into effective, efficient supply chain performance. Collaboration with operations teams helps category managers understand the practical implications of their sourcing decisions, such as **inventory management**, **supply chain disruptions**, and **quality control**. Operations can provide valuable input into the feasibility of supplier delivery timelines, and their involvement ensures that category strategies are aligned with operational realities.

A strong partnership with operations also enables category managers to identify potential **logistics** challenges, such as the need for specialized transportation or warehousing requirements. Furthermore, operations teams can assist in **supplier performance monitoring** by providing insights into issues such as product quality, on-time delivery, and service levels. Regular communication between category managers and operations ensures that category strategies are effectively executed and that any issues are addressed proactively.

Overcoming Internal Resistance to Change

One of the most significant challenges in implementing category management initiatives is overcoming **internal resistance to change**. Category management often involves a fundamental shift in how procurement is approached within an organization. The transition from traditional procurement practices to a more strategic, cross-functional approach can be met with resistance from stakeholders who are accustomed to familiar processes and systems.

Resistance to change can come from several sources. **Senior management** may be hesitant to invest in category management initiatives if they do not immediately see the value or if they are concerned about the cost of implementation. **Department heads** may be wary of giving up control over their procurement decisions, particularly if they feel that category management will reduce their autonomy or disrupt established relationships with suppliers. Additionally, **employees** who are used to working in silos or using traditional procurement methods may resist adopting new tools, processes, or ways of thinking.

To overcome this resistance, category managers must first focus on **clear communication**. Explaining the benefits of category management to internal stakeholders is key to gaining their support. It is essential to articulate how category management will improve procurement efficiency, reduce costs, enhance supplier relationships, and contribute to the organization's strategic objectives. By demonstrating that category management is not just about centralizing procurement but rather optimizing procurement for the benefit of the entire organization, category managers can help alleviate concerns.

Another way to overcome resistance is by involving key stakeholders early in the process. Engaging finance, legal, and operations teams in the development of category strategies ensures that they have a voice in shaping the direction of category management. This collaborative approach can increase buy-in and reduce the sense of **imposed change**. Additionally, providing training and resources to help employees understand the benefits and practical applications of category management can empower them to embrace the new way of working.

Finally, **celebrating early wins** is crucial to gaining traction and building momentum for category management initiatives. Demonstrating early success through measurable outcomes—such as cost savings, process improvements, or enhanced supplier performance—helps to build credibility and buy-in across the organization. As category management begins to deliver tangible results, resistance to change tends to diminish, and stakeholders become more supportive of the ongoing implementation.

Collaboration across the organization is fundamental to the success of category management. By building strong partnerships with finance, legal, operations, and other business functions, category managers can ensure that category strategies are comprehensive, aligned with organizational goals, and effectively executed. Overcoming internal resistance to change is an essential part of this process, and it requires clear communication, stakeholder engagement, and the demonstration of tangible results. With the right cross-functional collaboration, category management can become a powerful driver of organizational efficiency, cost savings, and long-term success.

Chapter 19: Future Trends in Category Management

As organizations continue to evolve in an increasingly complex global marketplace, category management is adapting to new dynamics shaped by technological advancements, shifting consumer demands, and the growing importance of sustainability and innovation. This chapter explores the future trends in category management, focusing on the increasing adoption of **agile procurement** and the growing role of **analytics** and **predictive insights** in shaping category strategies.

Agile Procurement and Category Management

Traditionally, procurement and category management have been rooted in structured processes and long-term planning. However, the fast-paced nature of the modern business environment, along with the disruptions caused by global events like the COVID-19 pandemic, has highlighted the need for greater flexibility and responsiveness in procurement strategies. **Agile procurement** is emerging as a key trend in category management, offering organizations the ability to adapt quickly to changing market conditions and customer needs.

Agility in category management emphasizes the ability to pivot and adjust strategies in response to external factors, such as supply chain disruptions, changes in consumer behavior, or shifts in industry regulations. Agile procurement involves **iterative planning**, continuous feedback loops, and **rapid decision-making** based on real-time data. This approach allows category managers to prioritize flexibility, ensuring that procurement strategies can evolve as circumstances change, rather than adhering strictly to long-term plans that may no longer be relevant.

In practice, agile procurement means that category managers will work in shorter cycles, focusing on delivering incremental value rather than committing to rigid multi-year contracts or long-term sourcing strategies. This might involve working with suppliers on more flexible terms, adapting to new technological innovations, and adopting an **iterative** approach to risk management. **Scrum methodologies**, which are commonly used in agile project management, are being adopted in procurement as well, with category teams working in sprints to achieve short-term goals while maintaining flexibility to adjust strategies as new information arises.

The **cross-functional collaboration** that is central to category management becomes even more important in an agile environment. Agile procurement requires closer collaboration between procurement, operations, finance, and other departments to quickly identify and act on emerging opportunities or threats. In this context, decision-making becomes more decentralized, with team members empowered to make decisions that align with overall organizational goals.

The **flexibility** and **speed** inherent in agile procurement are particularly valuable in industries where innovation cycles are short, and competitive pressures are intense. For example, in the technology or fashion industries, where trends can change rapidly, being able to quickly source materials or adjust procurement strategies can provide a significant competitive advantage. Agile procurement also allows organizations to be more responsive to **consumer demands**, ensuring that they can procure the right products at the right time, without overcommitting resources to long-term contracts or suppliers.

The Growing Role of Analytics and Predictive Insights

As businesses generate increasing amounts of data, the role of **analytics** and **predictive insights** in category management is becoming more significant. Advanced data analytics tools are helping category managers make more informed decisions by providing deeper insights into procurement patterns, supplier performance, market trends, and potential risks.

One of the most notable advancements in this area is the rise of **predictive analytics**, which leverages historical data and advanced algorithms to forecast future trends, demand patterns, and potential disruptions in the supply chain. Predictive insights allow category managers to anticipate changes in supply and demand, identify emerging risks before they become critical, and plan procurement strategies more effectively. For example, predictive analytics can help identify potential **supplier bottlenecks** or disruptions in the supply chain before they occur, allowing organizations to take proactive steps to mitigate risks.

The integration of **big data** and **machine learning** into category management is also transforming how category managers make decisions. By analyzing vast amounts of structured and unstructured data, organizations can gain a more comprehensive understanding of their suppliers, the market, and the broader business landscape. This wealth of information can be used to identify hidden patterns, assess supplier risk, evaluate opportunities for cost savings, and optimize inventory management.

Artificial intelligence (AI) and **machine learning** are playing an increasingly important role in predictive insights, allowing category managers to automate decision-making processes and improve procurement forecasting accuracy. AI-powered tools can analyze historical data to identify patterns and predict future outcomes, such as demand fluctuations or changes in commodity prices. This allows category managers to make data-driven decisions based on real-time insights, rather than relying solely on intuition or past experience.

Moreover, the role of **advanced analytics** in **supplier performance management** is becoming increasingly important. Category managers can now monitor supplier performance in real-time using analytics tools that track metrics such as on-time delivery, quality compliance, and cost competitiveness. This data can be used to make informed decisions about whether to continue, renegotiate, or end a supplier relationship. Predictive analytics can also be used to identify potential risks related to **supplier financial stability**, **geopolitical factors**, or **sustainability practices**, helping organizations mitigate risks before they affect the supply chain.

The ability to access and analyze real-time data also enables category managers to implement **dynamic pricing strategies** that adjust according to market conditions. By using predictive analytics to forecast price trends, category managers can make more informed decisions about when to negotiate contracts, adjust order quantities, or explore alternative suppliers. This is particularly valuable in industries where **commodity prices** are volatile or where **demand fluctuations** are difficult to predict.

The use of analytics also helps organizations to better understand the **total cost of ownership (TCO)** for different categories. By analyzing historical data, category managers can gain a clearer picture of the hidden costs associated with a category, such as transportation costs, inventory holding costs, or the costs of managing supplier relationships. This insight allows them to optimize procurement decisions, focusing on categories that offer the best value and long-term benefits for the organization.

Integrating Technology and Data-Driven Decision-Making

The future of category management is increasingly intertwined with technology, and this trend is expected to continue. The use of advanced **enterprise resource planning (ERP)** systems, **procurement platforms**, and **cloud-based solutions** is becoming more prevalent in category management processes. These technologies allow for seamless integration of data across various departments, enhancing collaboration and enabling real-time decision-making.

As procurement becomes more data-driven, organizations will invest in **cloud-based platforms** that allow category managers to access up-to-date information on suppliers, contracts, market conditions, and performance metrics. These platforms also enable category managers to integrate data from external sources, such as social media, news feeds, and market reports, to gain a more comprehensive view of the market.

Blockchain technology is another area that is expected to influence category management in the future. Blockchain can provide transparency and security in supply chain transactions, helping organizations track products from suppliers to end-users while reducing the risk of fraud and ensuring compliance with sustainability and ethical sourcing standards. As blockchain technology matures, it is likely to play a more prominent role in category management by providing a reliable way to verify the authenticity and traceability of goods.

The future of category management is marked by a shift toward greater agility, enhanced data-driven decision-making, and a deeper reliance on technology. **Agile procurement** offers organizations the flexibility to adapt quickly to changing market conditions, while the increasing use of **predictive analytics** allows category managers to make more informed, forward-thinking decisions. By embracing these trends, organizations can not only optimize their category management processes but also position themselves for long-term success in an ever-evolving business landscape. The integration of advanced technologies and data-driven insights will continue to shape the future of category management, driving **efficiency**, **cost savings**, and **competitive advantage**.

Emerging Challenges and Opportunities in Category Management

As category management continues to evolve in response to shifting market dynamics, technological advancements, and global trends, organizations face both emerging challenges and exciting opportunities. While category management presents a strategic framework for optimizing procurement and maximizing value, its future success depends on how effectively organizations navigate these challenges while seizing new opportunities for growth, efficiency, and innovation.

Emerging Challenges in Category Management

The landscape of category management is increasingly complex, and procurement professionals must address several emerging challenges to remain competitive.

1. Supply Chain Disruptions
Global supply chains have become more interconnected than ever, and with this interconnectedness comes greater vulnerability to disruptions. Events such as natural disasters, geopolitical instability, and the COVID-19 pandemic have highlighted the fragility of supply chains. For category managers, these disruptions pose significant risks to the timely procurement of goods and services, potentially leading to higher costs, delayed deliveries, and strained supplier relationships.

To mitigate these risks, category managers must build more **resilient supply chains** that can withstand unforeseen disruptions. This involves diversifying supplier bases, exploring nearshoring options, and employing advanced analytics to forecast potential risks. Additionally, more flexible procurement strategies, such as agile procurement, will allow category managers to quickly respond to changing circumstances.

2. Managing Supplier Risks

In a globalized market, category managers must contend with the growing risk of supplier instability. This includes issues such as financial difficulties, political and regulatory risks, environmental concerns, and ethical practices. The challenge for category managers is to identify potential risks within the supplier base and establish contingency plans to mitigate their impact.

With the increasing importance of **supply chain transparency**, category managers are under pressure to monitor supplier practices related to sustainability, human rights, and ethical sourcing. Ensuring that suppliers comply with standards of **corporate social responsibility** (CSR) and environmental regulations is an ongoing challenge that requires continuous vigilance and proactive engagement.

3. Integration of New Technologies

While technology offers immense opportunities for improving category management, the integration of new tools and platforms can be a daunting task. The transition to digital procurement, the adoption of **cloud-based systems**, and the implementation of **artificial intelligence** and **machine learning** require significant investment, training, and change management. Organizations must ensure that they have the necessary infrastructure, capabilities, and resources to successfully integrate these technologies into their category management strategies.

Moreover, with the rapid pace of technological change, category managers need to stay ahead of the curve in adopting emerging technologies. Failure to do so could result in inefficiencies, missed opportunities, and a loss of competitive advantage.

4. Data Privacy and Security Concerns

As category management becomes more data-driven, the volume of sensitive information being collected and shared across the supply chain increases. This presents a growing concern over data privacy and security. **Cybersecurity threats** are a significant risk for organizations, particularly as procurement functions become more reliant on digital platforms and third-party suppliers. Category managers must ensure that the data shared with suppliers, partners, and service providers is secure and complies with relevant privacy regulations, such as **GDPR** and other regional data protection laws.

5. Balancing Cost and Sustainability Goals

The drive for cost savings remains a central focus in category management, but there is an increasing pressure to balance these cost-saving objectives with sustainability and ethical sourcing requirements. Procurement professionals are faced with the challenge of finding suppliers that offer competitive pricing while also meeting stringent sustainability standards. This includes sourcing materials and products that are **environmentally friendly**, **ethically produced**, and **socially responsible**.

Finding the right balance between cost, quality, and sustainability can be difficult, as sustainable products and ethical sourcing practices may come with higher upfront costs. Category managers must work closely with internal stakeholders to align procurement goals with corporate sustainability initiatives and find ways to reduce environmental impact without sacrificing quality or performance.

6. Talent Shortages and Skill Gaps

The evolving nature of category management requires professionals with a diverse skill set that spans procurement, data analytics, technology, and strategic thinking. However, there is a growing shortage of skilled category managers and procurement professionals who possess the expertise to navigate these complex areas. The need for **upskilling** and **reskilling** procurement teams is critical to ensure that organizations can meet the challenges of modern category management.

As category management becomes more data-driven and technologically advanced, organizations must invest in training programs to ensure their teams have the skills to leverage new tools, analyze complex data, and implement innovative procurement strategies.

Emerging Opportunities in Category Management

While these challenges pose significant obstacles, they also present numerous opportunities for organizations to innovate and improve their category management practices.

1. Leveraging Advanced Analytics and Big Data

One of the most significant opportunities in category management is the ability to leverage advanced **data analytics** and **big data** to make more informed, data-driven decisions. By using predictive analytics and machine learning, category managers can gain deeper insights into supplier performance, market trends, and procurement risks. These insights enable them to make better purchasing decisions, optimize supplier relationships, and reduce costs.

Big data also helps category managers assess the **total cost of ownership** (TCO) for different categories, enabling them to optimize procurement strategies for long-term value rather than focusing solely on initial price. With the right data tools, category managers can identify hidden inefficiencies, uncover potential savings opportunities, and make procurement decisions that align with organizational goals.

2. Sustainable Procurement Practices
Sustainability has become a critical area of focus in procurement, with organizations increasingly looking to integrate **sustainable sourcing** practices into their category strategies. Category managers who embrace sustainability can unlock significant opportunities for value creation, including access to new markets, improved supplier relationships, and enhanced brand reputation.

Incorporating sustainability into category management strategies allows companies to address growing consumer demand for ethically produced goods and environmentally responsible practices. This can also help mitigate risks related to environmental regulations, supply chain disruptions, and reputational damage. By working closely with suppliers to improve sustainability practices, category managers can drive innovation, reduce waste, and enhance long-term profitability.

3. Technology as a Competitive Advantage
The integration of emerging technologies such as **artificial intelligence (AI), machine learning, blockchain**, and **cloud-based solutions** presents an opportunity for category managers to gain a competitive edge. These technologies enable real-time access to data, improved decision-making capabilities, and enhanced supply chain visibility.

For example, **blockchain technology** can enhance transparency and traceability in supply chains, providing a secure way to verify product authenticity and monitor supplier compliance with sustainability standards. Similarly, AI-powered tools can assist in **predictive forecasting**, helping category managers anticipate demand changes, optimize inventory levels, and negotiate better contracts with suppliers.

4. Collaboration and Strategic Partnerships

Category management offers an opportunity for organizations to forge **strategic partnerships** with suppliers, building long-term relationships that drive mutual value. By working closely with suppliers on joint innovation, sustainability initiatives, and cost-reduction strategies, category managers can create a more resilient and agile supply chain.

Additionally, collaboration within the organization is key to driving category management success. **Cross-functional teams** involving stakeholders from finance, legal, operations, and other departments can help ensure alignment between procurement strategies and broader business objectives. This cross-departmental collaboration leads to better decision-making, faster problem-solving, and more effective category management.

5. Talent Development and Leadership

The growing demand for skilled procurement professionals presents an opportunity for organizations to invest in talent development. By offering training and development programs, category managers can close the skills gap and ensure that their teams are equipped with the knowledge and tools needed to succeed in a rapidly changing procurement environment.

Fostering a culture of continuous learning and **leadership development** within the category management function also provides an opportunity to nurture future leaders who can drive innovation, foster collaboration, and contribute to the long-term success of the organization.

The challenges facing category management in the future are significant but manageable with the right strategies, tools, and mindset. By addressing supply chain risks, leveraging emerging technologies, adopting sustainable sourcing practices, and investing in talent development, category managers can turn these challenges into opportunities for growth and innovation. The evolving landscape of category management offers immense potential for organizations to enhance procurement performance, drive efficiency, and deliver greater value to their stakeholders. The key to success lies in the ability to adapt, collaborate, and stay ahead of the curve in an ever-changing market environment.

20. Building a Culture of Continuous Improvement in Category Management

As organizations continue to adopt category management as a strategic approach to procurement, the importance of fostering a culture of continuous improvement becomes paramount. A culture of continuous improvement not only drives the ongoing enhancement of procurement processes but also helps organizations adapt to changing market conditions, respond to evolving customer needs, and achieve long-term success. In category management, this culture is essential for refining strategies, enhancing supplier relationships, and ensuring sustained value creation.

The role of category managers in this context is crucial. They must lead efforts to promote a mindset of improvement, encourage innovation, and ensure that both successes and failures are used as learning opportunities. As the procurement function evolves, category managers must continuously adapt their strategies, processes, and tools to stay aligned with organizational goals while driving value.

Learning from Successes and Failures

Continuous improvement is driven by a commitment to learning, both from successes and from failures. In category management, evaluating past performance and extracting lessons from both achievements and shortcomings is essential for refining strategies and optimizing future outcomes.

1. Leveraging Successes
While failures offer important lessons, it is equally important to capitalize on successes. Celebrating achievements and recognizing what worked well can provide valuable insights into the strengths of the current category management approach. Whether a successful negotiation, a cost-saving initiative, or a sustainable sourcing achievement, identifying

the key drivers of success enables category managers to replicate and build upon these achievements.

A deep understanding of success factors, such as effective stakeholder collaboration, innovative procurement solutions, or strong supplier relationships, can inform future category strategies. Category managers can document best practices, share success stories across the organization, and create models for success that can be applied to other categories. This knowledge-sharing process helps standardize successful strategies and instills a sense of confidence and direction within procurement teams.

2. Embracing Failures as Learning Opportunities
Failures, although often difficult to confront, offer significant opportunities for learning and improvement. Whether a procurement strategy did not yield the expected savings, a supplier relationship broke down, or an implementation did not go as planned, category managers should foster an environment where these outcomes are viewed as stepping stones for growth rather than setbacks.

By analyzing the root causes of failures, category managers can identify weaknesses in processes, systems, or decision-making. Conducting post-mortem analyses and root cause analyses provides clarity on what went wrong and enables teams to develop corrective actions. Importantly, creating a culture where failures are not punished but seen as learning opportunities encourages openness, transparency, and a willingness to experiment with new approaches.

Category managers should also focus on improving risk management strategies to anticipate potential failures before they occur. By using data-driven insights, building more robust supplier relationships, and anticipating market changes, category managers can reduce the likelihood of failure while ensuring that when it does occur, it leads to valuable lessons.

Embedding Category Management in Organizational Culture

For category management to be truly effective, it must be embedded in the organization's culture. This means ensuring that category management principles are not only practiced by the procurement team but also understood and supported by all relevant stakeholders, including senior leadership, finance, operations, and other cross-functional teams.

1. Aligning Category Management with Organizational Goals

The first step in embedding category management in the organizational culture is to ensure that its objectives are closely aligned with the broader goals of the organization. When category management is linked to strategic business objectives such as cost reduction, revenue growth, sustainability, and operational efficiency, it gains greater visibility and support across the business.

Category managers should work closely with other departments, particularly finance and operations, to ensure that procurement strategies are integrated with business plans. By aligning category management initiatives with the company's overall strategy, category managers can demonstrate how their efforts contribute directly to the success of the organization.

2. Engaging Senior Leadership and Key Stakeholders

For category management to thrive, it requires buy-in from senior leadership and key stakeholders. Top-level executives must recognize the strategic value of category management and be willing to invest in the necessary resources, tools, and training. When senior leadership champions category management, it signals to the rest of the organization that procurement is not just a tactical function but a key driver of business success.

Engaging stakeholders from across the organization ensures that category management strategies are aligned with the needs and priorities of various departments. Cross-functional collaboration fosters a sense of shared responsibility for category management outcomes, creating a more integrated approach to procurement. Regular communication and collaboration with stakeholders help identify new opportunities for improvement, streamline processes, and ensure that category management remains aligned with evolving business objectives.

3. Promoting a Collaborative Mindset

To embed category management in organizational culture, it is essential to foster a collaborative mindset across the business. Category managers should encourage open communication and knowledge-sharing with other departments, breaking down silos and promoting joint problem-solving. When category managers work closely with marketing, finance, IT, and operations teams, they can better understand the broader needs of the organization and create category strategies that drive cross-functional value.

This collaboration helps identify potential challenges early in the process, align procurement strategies with operational realities, and ensure that everyone is working toward the same goals. A culture of collaboration also supports innovation, as different perspectives and expertise can help generate new ideas and solutions that enhance category management performance.

The Evolving Role of the Category Manager

As category management continues to evolve, the role of the category manager is also transforming. Category managers are no longer just tactical buyers; they have become strategic partners within the organization. Their role encompasses a wide range of responsibilities, from strategic sourcing and supplier relationship management to data analysis and risk management.

1. Strategic Leadership and Decision Making
Category managers are increasingly being called upon to provide strategic leadership in procurement. They are expected to not only manage the day-to-day operations of their categories but also to contribute to long-term business strategy. This requires a deep understanding of market dynamics, supply chain risks, and organizational goals. Category managers must make data-driven decisions, weigh competing priorities, and guide their teams in executing strategies that align with overall business objectives.

As the strategic role of category managers grows, they must also be able to communicate effectively with senior leadership, providing insights and recommendations that drive business performance. This requires strong leadership skills, business acumen, and the ability to influence stakeholders at all levels.

2. Embracing Digital Transformation
The increasing adoption of digital technologies in procurement is reshaping the role of category managers. From artificial intelligence and machine learning to cloud-based procurement platforms, digital tools are enabling category managers to make more informed decisions, automate repetitive tasks, and gain deeper insights into supplier performance.

Category managers must stay ahead of the curve by embracing digital transformation and leveraging technology to drive procurement excellence. This includes using predictive analytics for demand forecasting, automating contract management processes, and implementing advanced spend analysis tools. Embracing these tools will allow category managers to focus on higher-value strategic tasks while improving the efficiency and accuracy of procurement operations.

3. Developing New Skills and Capabilities

As category management becomes more complex and multifaceted, category managers must continuously develop new skills to stay competitive. This includes expertise in data analytics, supplier risk management, sustainability practices, and advanced negotiation techniques. The evolving role of category managers requires them to be lifelong learners, constantly updating their knowledge and skills to keep up with changes in technology, market conditions, and organizational needs.

Professional development programs, mentoring, and collaboration with other procurement leaders are essential to the growth of category managers. By investing in training and development, organizations can ensure that their category managers have the capabilities to meet future challenges and seize new opportunities.

Building a culture of continuous improvement in category management requires a strategic commitment to learning, collaboration, and adaptation. By learning from both successes and failures, embedding category management within the organizational culture, and evolving the role of the category manager, organizations can drive ongoing improvements in procurement performance. The category manager's role as a strategic leader, coupled with a strong culture of improvement, will help organizations navigate the complexities of modern procurement, deliver value across the supply chain, and ensure long-term success.

Glossary of Key Terms

Category Management: A strategic approach to procurement where spending on products and services is grouped into categories, and specific strategies are developed for each category to optimize value for the organization.

Spend Analysis: The process of analyzing an organization's spending data to identify trends, opportunities for cost savings, and strategic sourcing initiatives.

Total Cost of Ownership (TCO): A financial estimate designed to help organizations determine the total cost of a product or service over its entire lifecycle, including acquisition, operation, and disposal costs.

Strategic Sourcing: The process of identifying, evaluating, and selecting suppliers based on their ability to provide goods or services that align with the organization's strategic objectives.

Kraljic Matrix: A strategic tool used to assess the importance of different procurement categories based on supply risk and the impact on an organization's financial performance.

Supplier Relationship Management (SRM): A strategic approach to managing an organization's interactions with its suppliers, aimed at developing long-term, mutually beneficial relationships.

Key Performance Indicators (KPIs): Quantifiable metrics used to assess the success of category management strategies and the performance of suppliers.

Risk Management: The process of identifying, assessing, and mitigating risks that could negatively affect an organization's ability to meet its procurement objectives.

Digital Transformation: The integration of digital technology into all areas of procurement, changing how organizations operate and deliver value to customers and stakeholders.

Agile Procurement: A procurement approach that focuses on flexibility, iterative progress, and the ability to quickly respond to changing business and market conditions.

Practical Tools and Templates

Category Management Framework Template
A structured template outlining the key components of category management, including spend analysis, supplier identification, category segmentation, and strategy development. It serves as a guide to develop tailored procurement strategies for each category.

Spend Analysis Template
A spreadsheet template that helps procurement teams categorize and analyze spending data, enabling the identification of cost-saving opportunities and the prioritization of categories that require focused attention.

Supplier Evaluation Matrix
A tool for assessing potential suppliers based on criteria such as cost, quality, delivery, and sustainability. This template helps category managers make informed decisions when selecting suppliers.

Kraljic Matrix Template
A visual tool to assess procurement categories based on their risk and impact on the organization's profitability. It helps prioritize sourcing strategies and categorize suppliers into strategic, leverage, bottleneck, and non-critical groups.

Category Strategy Plan Template
A document template for outlining specific strategies for each procurement category. It includes objectives, key initiatives, timelines, and responsible parties, ensuring alignment with organizational goals.

Risk Management Template
A comprehensive template for identifying, evaluating, and mitigating risks in procurement. It includes risk categories, likelihood assessments, impact analysis, and mitigation strategies.

Category Performance Dashboard
A visual tool to track and report category management performance metrics, such as cost savings, supplier performance, and compliance to contracts. It helps category managers monitor progress and identify areas for improvement.

Real-World Case Studies

Case Study: Manufacturing Sector – Strategic Sourcing for Raw Materials
A leading manufacturing company faced rising raw material costs and inconsistent supplier performance. Through effective category management, the company implemented a strategic sourcing initiative, negotiated long-term contracts with key suppliers, and adopted a

collaborative supplier management approach. As a result, the company achieved significant cost savings, improved material quality, and reduced supply chain risks.

Case Study: Retail Industry – Streamlining Supplier Relationships

A global retail chain utilized category management to overhaul its supplier relationships. By segmenting categories based on strategic importance and supplier risk, the retailer focused on building strong, long-term partnerships with key suppliers while optimizing performance in lower-priority categories. This strategy led to improved supplier collaboration, more efficient inventory management, and enhanced product availability.

Case Study: Healthcare Sector – Managing High-Value Categories

A healthcare provider implemented category management for its medical device procurement. By conducting thorough market analysis and leveraging spend data, the organization was able to negotiate better pricing and terms with suppliers. The result was a reduction in overall procurement costs, improved supply chain reliability, and enhanced patient care due to more timely access to critical medical supplies.

Case Study: Government Procurement – Risk Management and Compliance

A government agency faced procurement challenges with high-risk categories, such as IT services and consulting. Through effective category management, the agency implemented a risk-based approach, addressing compliance issues, supplier performance, and long-term contract management. This approach improved transparency, reduced procurement risks, and ensured compliance with regulatory standards.

References and Further Reading

Monczka, R. M., Handfield, R. B., Giunipero, L. C., & Patterson, J. L. (2015). *Purchasing and Supply Chain Management* (6th ed.). Cengage Learning.
This book offers in-depth insights into supply chain and procurement management, covering key topics such as supplier selection, contract management, and strategic sourcing.

Kraljic, P. (1983). "Purchasing must become supply management." *Harvard Business Review*, 61(5), 109-117.
This seminal article introduces the Kraljic Matrix, which has since become a cornerstone of category management practices, especially for strategic sourcing.

CIPS (Chartered Institute of Procurement and Supply). *Category Management in Procurement and Supply*.
CIPS provides valuable guidelines, frameworks, and best practices for procurement professionals looking to implement category management effectively.

Christopher, M. (2016). *Logistics and Supply Chain Management* (5th ed.). Pearson Education.
Christopher's book covers supply chain management practices and emphasizes the importance of integrating category management into supply chain strategies.

Cousins, P. D., Lamming, R. C., & Bowen, F. (2004). *The Lean Supply Chain: Managing the Challenge at Tesco.* Pearson Education.
This book delves into the application of lean principles in category management, offering practical examples from leading global companies.

Index

A

- Agile Procurement, 332-334
- Automation in Procurement, 180-185
- Analytical Tools for Category Management, 132-135

B

- Benefits of Category Management, 35-40
- Best Practices in Category Strategy, 82-87
- Big Data in Procurement, 257-260

C

- Collaborative Procurement, 218-222

- Continuous Improvement in Category Management, 345-350
- Cost Savings through Category Management, 56-60
- Cross-functional Collaboration, 127-130

D

- Digital Transformation in Procurement, 143-148
- Data-Driven Decision Making, 140-142
- Demand Forecasting in Category Management, 200-204

E

- Ethical Sourcing, 290-295
- E-Procurement Tools, 161-165
- Evaluation of Suppliers, 120-122

F

- Framework for Category Management, 75-78
- Financial Implications of Category Management, 63-67
- Forecasting in Category Management, 112-115

G

- Global Category Management, 305-310
- Glossary of Key Terms, 415-420

H

- High-Value Categories, 205-210
- How to Implement Category Strategies, 90-95
- Holistic Approach to Category Management, 85-88

www.ingramcontent.com/pod-product-compliance
Lightning Source LLC
Chambersburg PA
CBHW071026240526
45469CB00006BD/2115